**DO NOT REMOVE
CARDS FROM POCKET**

THE RITES OF WINTER

A Skier's Budget Guide to Making It on the Slopes

Bruce Jacobsen
and
Rollin Riggs

PRIAM BOOKS

ARBOR HOUSE
New York

Bruce dedicates this book to Julie Williams.
Rollin dedicates it to Lynn.
And we both want to express our appreciation to the members of
the National Ski Patrol, whose service to the ski industry is an
inspiration.

Copyright © 1984 by Rollin Riggs and Bruce Jacobsen

Library of Congress Cataloging in Publication Data

Jacobsen, Bruce.
The rites of winter.

1. Skis and skiing—United States—Guide-books.
2. United States—Description and travel—1981-   —Guide-books. I. Riggs,
Rollin. II. Title.
GV854.4.J23   1984   917.3   84–18453
ISBN 0-87795-640-5 (alk. paper)

Manufactured in the United States of America
10 9 8 7 6 5 4 3 2 1

This book is printed on acid free paper. The paper in this book meets the
guidelines for permanence and durability of the Committee on Production
Guidelines for Book Longevity of the Council on Library Resources.

CONTENTS

2250859

ACKNOWLEDGMENTS

A number of people helped make this book possible. First, we'd like to thank our researchers, all of whom came through in the clutch: Mike Natan, Hal Kalechofsky, Ann Creighton, Lisa Gosselin, Donna Kositz, and Chris Plakos.

Kathe Dillman at the National Ski Areas Association helped us start this avalanche, and a number of great folks at each mountain made us feel very welcome: Jack Brendlinger, Geri Wright, Pamela Stenmark, Joe Macy, Chris Stagg, Pete French, Dave Anderson, Jane Dunham, Gay Porter Byerly, Paul Heard, Dick Courcelle, Jeff Lathrop, Dick May, Debbi Moore, Packy Longfellow, Susan Appleby, and Polly Rollins.

Further, a bunch of friends provided moral support, companionship, and sometimes cash: Joy Harris, Eric Kampmann, Lisa Kovitz, Kathy Edrington, Walt Little (who bought the beer book), Bubski Cutler, Feathers Maizes, Studley Marcus, Caitlin Doyle, Dana Martin, Dave Rachlin, Mrs. Marian Williams of Gray Rock Sales Associates, Melissa Paley, and Chris Ostapowicz.

Finally, our deepest gratitude goes to our parents, Arthur and Elizabeth Jacobsen and Webster and Sandy Riggs.

Bruce Jacobsen
Rollin Riggs

May, 1984

INTRODUCTION

Making this book was tough—racing down Jackson Hole's powdery runs, checking out Aspen's glamorous bars, drinking hot toddies by the fire at Killington . . . believe it, we earned our money!

And in the course of our research, we not only discovered ways to help you save on your next ski trip, we also hit upon the answer to the burning question: "What's the difference between all those ski resorts, anyway?"

There are dozens of books on how to ski but none on *where* to ski. If you're looking for the gentle mountains where beginners can learn with ease, or challenging mountains that won't make you look like a fool, we've got them. If huge moguls, sheer drops and shoulder-deep powder are more your style, we'll tell you where to go. Looking for a quiet vacation in the mountains, with a little skiing and a lot of relaxing? Want to ski, drink and dance with the cowboys and the jet set? We've been there, too.

So, this book is for skiers of all levels and tastes who want to understand the differences between Purgatory and Telluride, or Sugarbush and Sugarloaf—and want to save a little money. We'll suggest *reasonably* priced restaurants and lodging—because while we all know that skiing is an expensive sport (few of the resorts are really convenient, the equipment is costly, and the day of the $10 lift ticket is long gone) we don't see any reason to stay in a room on the slopes for $100 a night when a room one block away costs $50.

Each chapter includes an overall description of the resort—what the town looks like, whom the mountain is designed for, and who skis there. We couldn't begin to cram in all the many different airline packages, holiday deals, midweek specials, and other complicated rate structures that each ski area and each hotel has to offer, so it's best to consult the resort's central reservations office. Most resorts have a toll-free number and an extremely knowledgeable staff to assist callers, and many of these central reservation services will arrange airport pickup, lodging, equipment rental, lessons, and any extra skiing reservations you may need. Chambers of Commerce at the larger towns can supply you with information about activities other than skiing in the area.

When planning your trip, keep some of these points in mind:

1. The prices we quote were good for the 1983–84 season and are usually nonholiday rates. Unless otherwise indicated the price given for lift tickets is the one-day charge for adults during

regular season. Children's and half-day tickets (which are usually good after 1:00 P.M.) are normally 30 to 50 percent less. All resorts offer a discount for multiple-day passes as well.

2. Prices are lowest in early December, January, and April. They drop in January, the middle of the season, because in the East it gets really cold, and in the West ski conditions are often below par. But if you can bundle up and the snow has been good, January is a great time to save money and avoid crowds.

3. Bargaining will often reduce your cost at many ski lodges. It's pretty tough to bargain during weekends or holidays and it won't work at large hotels unless you've got a big group, but the smaller places are sometimes willing to negotiate and during the week it's worth a try.

4. For the more expensive establishments use a reservation service. At smaller areas, the service will keep in touch with all the inns, but at larger ones, they often just negotiate with the big lodges because of the better commissions. But, if you ask, any service should at least tell you the name of a dormitory.

5. Exercise caution with the weather. If you're driving, make sure to pack some food and first-aid gear, just in case you get stranded in a snowstorm. When you're on the mountain, take precautions against frostbite, sunburn, and windburn. Remember, it takes less alcohol to get drunk at high altitudes, so be aware of your limits.

Some of the terms we use in the book might be a bit foreign to novices, so we'll explain a few here. Ski trails are divided into novice, intermediate, and expert classes. Novice trails are designated by green colors and a circle; intermediate runs by blue colors and a square; expert by black colors and a diamond. Remember, each mountain has its own designations of difficulty. They cannot be universally applied. An "intermediate" run at Taos might be rated "expert" someplace else. In general, expert runs are known for their moguls or "bumps," those large mounds of snow packed close together which can take years to navigate gracefully.

Please remember the problem that all travel guides face: by the time the book is out, some of the businesses have closed, new places have opened, and some facts, prices, phone numbers, etc. have changed. This is especially true of ski areas, which are always adding new lifts, cutting new trails, etc. We can say this: as of May, 1984, all our information was correct.

Also, of course, we are mere mortals, and we can make mistakes. We've probably overlooked some great bars, or raved about some restaurants that you hate. And there are some smaller ski areas that we would have liked to cover, but just didn't have time for. However, we do think that this book lays an excellent foundation, and, as we hope to revise it every two years or so, we would certainly appreciate your input: Did we steer you wrong? Did we miss something you love or hate? Did we do something right? (A pat on the back is always appreciated.) Please let us know how we can improve this book in the future. A guide's best researchers should be its readers, so keep in touch. You can write to us in care of the publisher.

One more thing. The word *après-ski* is an abomination, and this is the first and last time you will see it in this book. Do teachers make children stay *après-school?* Do you go to a movie *après-dinner?* Of course not. Please join us in our little battle to eradicate this linguistic menace from American ski resorts.

Skiing is the second most fun activity that mankind has ever devised. With only a little practice you can experience great exercise and unequaled thrills, all amidst spectacular scenery. What more could you ask for?

And contrary to popular belief, participation in this sport does not require a second mortgage on the house or a winning lottery ticket. In the following pages we'll show you that a ski vacation can be very affordable. This book, however, is not a complete directory to *every* facility at *every* major ski resort in the country. Instead, we hope it will serve as a guide, a means of comparison shopping to save you time and money at home and at the resort. So go discover the mountain of your choice.

See you on the slopes!

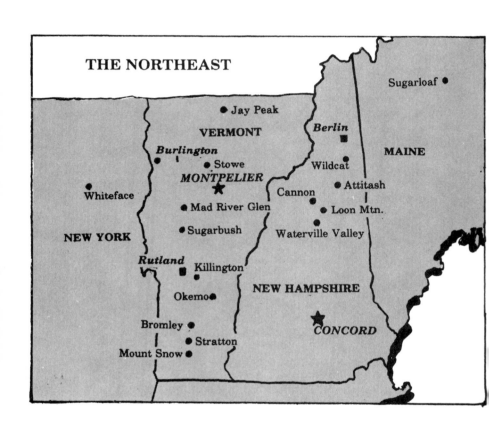

THE NORTHEAST

Sugarloaf ●

● Jay Peak

VERMONT   Berlin ■

Burlington   MAINE
     ● Stowe   Wildcat ●
MONTPELIER ★   Cannon   ● Attitash
              ●
● Mad River Glen   ● Loon Mtn.

Whiteface

● Sugarbush   Waterville Valley

NEW YORK

Rutland ● Killington
      ■
                    NEW HAMPSHIRE
   Okemo ●

Bromley ●   CONCORD ★
   ● Stratton
Mount Snow ●

New England

In the good old days, skiing in New England was for the rugged out-doorsman who'd hike up the trails and ski down between rocks and trees. Today, skiing is a major industry, and ski resorts cater to every-body—from young urban professionals in their Saabs to busloads of beginners from Brooklyn. In the process, many mountains have lost their rustic, hardy atmosphere, and skiing is no longer the sport of the intrepid individualist.

Eastern resorts are tougher to compare than western areas. East-ern resorts are much smaller and their nightlife is minimal in compari-son. Most folks drive to eastern ski areas, so the major decision is whether one mountain is worth another hour or two in the car.

For our money, it's best to head farther north. Areas like Stowe and Mad River have better snow, bigger mountains, and more atmo-sphere. Stowe is one of the oldest areas around, and one of the big-gest. There's a wide range of trails, including some of New England's hardest as well as beginner and intermediate trails. Mad River and Sugarbush team up to provide some of the best skiing around: Sugar-bush is incredibly slick and crowded, but still a great mountain; Mad River, on the other hand, has preserved the old New England style, and has some of the most challenging runs around. Between these two resorts you'll find what may be New England's liveliest night life. And with the new discount air travel to Burlington, these resorts can be an inexpensive plane ride away.

Killington may start its own *Guinness Book of New England Ski Records:* it has the most skiers, the longest trails, the most snowmak-ing, and the longest season. At Killington, skiing is the number-one industry—and a very well-managed one at that.

Farther south, Bromley and Stratton offer good skiing closer to home. Their mountains aren't nearly as long or as difficult as their neighbors to the north, but they work hard on their slopes and attract big crowds. Their nightlife isn't sizzling, but families will enjoy towns like Manchester and the variety of things to do. Okemo is trying to become a major resort, but the results aren't in yet, while Mount Snow, purchased by Killington, has shown great results.

If you really want to escape from it all, go way north to Jay Peak or Sugarloaf. The crowds are smaller and the nightlife quieter. In size and number of trails, the mountains fit in somewhere between Stowe and Stratton. Or head west to Whiteface. There's a lot more there than skiing—an Olympic bobsled run, a speed-skating rink, etc.

New Hampshire ski resorts are generally smaller and less developed than those in Vermont. Waterville Valley is friendly and draws heavily from Massachusetts. Its mostly intermediate slopes attract more day-skiers than overnight visitors and just up the road is the fast-growing Loon, which is Waterville's overflow area and still too small to warrant its own chapter. Cannon is vintage New England: tough, steep, and frequently windy and icy. The Mount Washington Valley offers two major ski areas and two minor ones: Attitash, with its sophisticated snowmaking equipment and limited lift-ticket sales, makes fine use of somewhat scarce resources; and Wildcat offers challenging terrain, a big mountain, and a ringside seat to the "world's worst weather" on Mount Washington. The two smaller areas, Mount Cranmore and Black Mountain, handle the overflow from Attitash and Wildcat.

SUGARLOAF

To compensate for the fact that Sugarloaf is in the middle of Maine and five hours from everything, the designers of this ski resort have gone out of their way to insure that once you get out of your car, you won't get back in until it's time to leave. Though the mountain is big (it has the third longest vertical drop in the East), the living is compact and convenient. In the village, next to the gondola and lifts, you'll find a half-dozen restaurants, a spa, bank, grocery/liquor store, laundromat, two nightspots with live music, ski shops, etc.

This compactness not only saves you money on gas, it also means you don't have to be outside very much at night—and Maine in the winter is freezing. Hell, Maine in the *summer* is freezing. So come prepared to battle severe cold and frostbite. Lodging on the slopes has also given Sugarloaf a reputation as a "skier's mountain"—trailside living coupled with very short lift lines make for full days of skiing.

THE SKIING

With an even balance of diamonds, squares, and circles, Sugarloaf appeals to the full range of skiers. For the expert, the area boasts the only lift-serviced snowfield skiing in the East (usually open only in the

spring) but since there are no top-to-bottom expert trails, the mountain is best suited to the intermediate.

All fifty trails begin at one peak, ending at or near the base lodge. This makes for convenient skiing without much traversing. The expert trails are all at the top third of the mountain, and the lifts and T-bars near the peak segregate the experts from the novices. Of the expert trails, the aptly named Upper Widowmaker, Babblecuffer, and Boom Auger are among the most difficult.

You'll find the best skiing on the three-mile Binder, Tote Road, and Double Bitter trails. Mostly intermediate, these runs cut serpentine paths through the forest to the base lodge. An occasional mogul and some steep drops keep the skier alert, and the easy sections interspersed throughout let everyone enjoy the fine view of the surrounding mountains.

If you're too impatient for the five-minute lift wait, take the Bucksaw Chair on the west side, or the long Wiffletree T-bar on the east side. The longest wait you'll have is for the gondola—twenty minutes on a very busy weekend.

Because it's so far north, Sugarloaf's conditions are better than those of its southern neighbors. Unlike some mountains, most of Sugarloaf's runs aren't windblown, and have a sunny exposure, which means you can ski as easily in the afternoon as in the morning. This, along with the more northerly clime, means that Sugarloaf gets more snow (and holds it better) than many other areas.

THE TOWN/NIGHTLIFE

Let's put it simply: if you can't make it to one of the three or so good bars, get ready for a night of Trivial Pursuit by the fireplace. The two towns nearby, Stratton (eight miles north) and Kingfield (sixteen miles south) are not Aspen—or even Camden, New Jersey, for that matter.

On the mountain, you have two choices: Maxwell's, a bawdy, college-oriented bar, and Gepetto's, a restaurant/bar that caters to the older, more mellow crowd. Both spots feature live music nearly every night. On weekend nights, Maxwell's serves up the most beer this side of Fort Lauderdale, and if you want a few on weekends, get there early—it's usually packed before 11:00 P.M. Swap that beer for a brandy or a carafe of wine at Gepetto's, where the more relaxed crowd enjoys mellow folk music. If you time it right, you can be eating dinner just as the music starts.

Once off the mountain, aside from the Red Snapper, a slightly inferior clone of Maxwell's, and D. F. Scribrer's, a local hangout featuring a pool table, you quickly realize you're in Kingfield, Maine. In other words, Deadsville. The nearest movie theater is a half-hour away! (But those staying on the mountain have access to Sugarloaf TV, which shows first-run movies at night. Plus, there's wall after wall of video games in the village.)

4

RESTAURANTS

There are, however, a variety of dining options right on the mountain, all a snowball's throw from the base lodge. For European cuisine served by candlelight, dine at the Truffle Hound. The menu includes duck and veal, as well as appetizers like pâté and escargots. Meals run $15 per person. The Chinese food at Lita's is reasonably priced at approximately $8 per person. Szechuan and Cantonese styles are highlighted, with luncheon specials available ($4.75). A Winter Harbor specializes in fresh seafood, such as lobster, shrimp, scallops, and swordfish. The raw bar is a popular spot in the afternoon. It will cost about $10 per person. The Sugarloaf Inn Resort serves fine entrees and exotic desserts like Amaretto Nut Mousse, all for approximately $13. Gepetto's, mentioned earlier, specializes in Italian cuisine, though it also serves fresh Maine seafood. The atmosphere is more casual here, but it will still cost you around $10 for your dinner.

Most of these restaurants serve lunch as well; they are vastly superior to the lodge cafeteria. For between $4 and $5, you'll get a good lunch at A Winter Harbor, Gepetto's, Sugarloaf Inn, or Lita's. Of the mountainside eateries, only The Bag was disappointing, with food and service well below par.

Out of the village and down the mountain road is One Stanley Avenue, a beautiful Victorian house that offers excellent Maine cuisine. The ambiance at The Winter's Inn is similar, and its French cuisine is superb. At $15 per plate, it represents the expensive side of the off-mountain dining.

On the less expensive side is Macho's Hacienda, with good Mexican food at $7 per person, or The Chateau, with cheap but tasty pizzas, subs, and pasta.

LODGING

To fully benefit from Sugarloaf, you must stay on the mountain, and the first and best option for the budget-minded is the mountain's condos. All come equipped with modern kitchens, new furniture, fireplaces, and other amenities. Sizes and prices vary, but all are spacious enough to sleep a few extra in the living room. You can bring a few sacks of food and prepare meals in your condo—the grocery can provide what you forget. Most condos are available through Mountainside Condominiums, which has a good package deal: three-and-a-half days, three nights, lift tickets, lessons, and a bottle of wine, all for $99 (midweek, double occupancy).

Peter Webber's Inn, a full-service hotel, is another option. A chairlift ride from the base lodge, the hotel has forty-four beautifully furnished rooms. The Inn offers a midwinter, midweek package of five days/five nights for $184 per person. This includes lodging (two per bedroom) and lift tickets.

Once you're off the mountain you pay less, and get less. The Lumberjack Lodge, a huge house, has cozy rooms, a sauna and a TV/game room with rent starting at $18. Judson's features breakfast, lunch, and dinner (all cooked by Ma Judson), and rates begin at $20. At The Chateau, you can get a room as cheaply as humanly possible ($12 or so), but you sacrifice material comforts like space and private bathrooms.

For other bargains try The Widow's Walk in Stratton, a Victorian home that costs $25 per night with meals, and also in Stratton, the Mountain View, which starts at $14 per person. The Country Cupboard in Kingfield costs $22 for bed and breakfast. Sugarloafer's Ski Dorm, a unique log-fort dormitory, starts at $8.50 per person.

The Winter's Inn is a classic mansion starting at $40 per person and the Herbert Motel, though perhaps not classic, is cheap at $10 per person.

ACCESSIBILITY

Sugarloaf is 230 miles from Boston. Augusta, Bangor (both one hour away), and Portland (two hours away) have airports, and you'll have to rent a car to get to the mountain. There is no bus service in the area.

LISTINGS

Sugarloaf/USA
Carrabassett Valley
Kingfield, ME   04947
207-237-2861

LIFT TICKET

$21

RESTAURANTS

A Winter Harbor, 237-2000.
The Bag, 237-2451.
Gepetto's, 237-2192.
Maxwell's, 237-2000.
Lita's, 237-2402.
Sugarloaf Inn Resort, 237-2701.
The Truffle Hound, 237-2355.
One Stanley Avenue, Kingfield, 265-5541.
The Winter's Inn, Kingfield, 265-5421.
Macho's Hacienda, Route 27, 235-2421.

The Chateau, Carrabassett Valley, 235-2731.

LODGING

Mountain Side Condominiums, 237-2000 or toll-free 800-451-0002.
Sugarloaf Inn, 237-2701 or 800-434-4075.
Lumberjack Lodge, Carrabassett Valley, 237-2141.
The Chateau, Carrabassett Valley, 235-2731.
Judson's, Carrabassett Valley, 235-2641.
The Widow's Walk, Stratton, 246-6901.
Arnold Trail Inn, Stratton, 246-2000.
Mountain View Motel, Stratton, 246-2922.
Country Cupboard, Kingfield, 265-2193.
Sugarloafer's Ski Dorm, Kingfield, 265-2041.
Winter's Inn, Kingfield, 265-5421.
Herbert Hotel, Kingfield, 265-2000.

CANNON
MOUNTAIN

If you're looking for the quintessential New England ski experience, you may find it at Cannon—cold, windy, icy, steep, and crowded on the weekends, with a tiny, quaint town just down the road.

Cannon is the oldest major ski resort in the East, with a mountain New Englanders thrive on. The wind at the peak blasts the snow cover off the ice, but even so the top never shuts down. Cannon, the northernmost ski area on the "Ski 93" circuit, offers some fine trails and usually smaller crowds than its neighbors. But if you're not the truly hardy type, Cannon may just make you miserable.

THE SKIING

The eighty-passenger tramway carries skiers 5,350 feet in six minutes. On peak weekends and during holiday periods, a pass for the tramway will add $3 to your lift ticket—and the tram gets very crowded. But the views are spectacular, and once you disembark you'll have the entire mountain to enjoy. You'll find the intermediate trails at the peak challenging—they're icy and steep, and the wind whips around you. There's snowmaking on the runs below the tram building but not on those off to the right, and these slopes are ridiculous when there hasn't been any snow for a while.

At the middle of the mountain, the trails become wider and great for bombing. You'll encounter some tricky turns on the Lower Ravine, while showboats enjoy the small hills on Lower Cannon.

Experts should veer to the left and tackle one of four short runs that lead to either lift B or the tram. Of these steep, moguled trails, only Rocket has snowmaking, and it's wonderful. Intermediates can take Gary's on this route, but if conditions are good, they should try Rocket or Paulie's Folly, too.

The runs to the bottom lifts are fine for beginners and a lot of fun to bomb. Beginners also have a "Pony Lift" and their own small trail on the far right of the base area.

Overall, Cannon offers some very fine skiing for such a small mountain. The transportation system—three double chairs, two T-bars, and the tram—is good, and the terrain is diverse and especially challenging for the intermediate. Ordinarily, two days at Cannon is plenty,

unless you're trying to escape the crowds at Waterville Valley and Loon.

THE TOWN/LODGING

While there is no lodging at the mountain, three miles away is the sleepy, picturesque little town of Franconia. Although it has next to nothing in the way of nightlife, you'll discover some lovely little inns that are most conducive to getting warm and relaxed and sipping a hot drink by the fire.

The one small restaurant in town, The Dutch Treat, serves good Italian food as well as standard diner fare. It shows movies there as well a few nights a week.

Most skiers, however, eat and drink at the inns.

Quiet and lovely and just the right size, the Franconia Inn has twenty-nine rooms furnished with antiques, and a renowned dining room and lounge. Another asset is the ski touring center next door. Rooms cost between $45 and $56.

The Hillwinds, the Stonybrook, Raynor's, and the Gale River are the major motels in the area. With thirty rooms each, the Hillwinds and Raynor's are the largest, but all four are really comparable. The

Stonybrook is closest to the lifts, and the Hillwinds' dining room serves good steaks, plus they have an enormous lounge where you can listen to live music most nights. All cost around $20 to $40 a night.

Lovett's Inn is a charming, rambling place with rooms, cottages, and duplexes. Rates are in the $35 to $60 range, and their three-day package, which includes breakfast and dinner, starts at $80.

The Sunset Hill House, two miles west of Franconia in Sugar Hill, is another lovely inn that offers great New England cuisine. It's in the $50 range.

To find out about the package deals, contact the Franconia Chamber of Commerce. You can get a lift ticket at a reduced price, a room, and breakfast and dinner, starting at $90 or so for three days.

ACCESSIBILITY

Cannon Mountain is right off I-93—three hours from Boston, six from New York. The town of Franconia is three miles north of the ski area. Burlington, Vermont and Manchester, New Hampshire both have major airports and are about an hour and a half away. Trailways has bus service to Franconia.

LISTINGS

Cannon Mountain
Franconia, NH   03580
603-823-5563

Franconia Chamber of Commerce
Franconia, NH   03580
603-823-5661

LIFT TICKET

$16 (On weekends and holidays, a lift ticket is $17, plus a $3 surcharge for the use of the tram.)

LODGING AND RESTAURANTS

The Dutch Treat Restaurant, Main Street, 823-8851.
The Franconia Inn, Route 116, Easton Road, 823-5542.
The Hillwinds Motel, Route 18, Main Street, 823-5551.
The Stonybrook Motor Lodge, Route 18, 823-8192.
Raynor's Motor Lodge, Routes 18 and 142, 823-5651.
Gale River Motel, Route 18, 823-5655.
Lovett's Inn, Route 18, Profile Road, 823-7761.
The Sunset Hill House, in Sugar Hill, 823-5522.

MOUNT WASHINGTON VALLEY: ATTITASH AND WILDCAT

Of the four ski areas in the Mount Washington Valley—Attitash, Wildcat, Mount Cranmore, and Black Mountain—Attitash and Wildcat are the most prominent. Attitash and Wildcat are major league, while Cranmore and Black Mountain are second string. Head for the little guys when Attitash and Wildcat are full.

Although close to one another, Attitash seems newer and more innovative than Wildcat. Wildcat is bigger than Attitash (and colder), and while most of Attitash could be skied in a day, it would take two to cover Wildcat. Wildcat's terrain is much more challenging, in part because less snowmaking means more ice.

Unlike the other major ski areas in New Hampshire, these mountains also have a large, bustling town a few miles away. Dozens of restaurants and motels, plus a few decent bars, make the town of North Conway a pocket of commercialism nestled in the rural grace of the valley. Some people avoid the town; others must force themselves to stop shopping and go skiing. One other thing sets Washington Valley apart—the cross-country skiing. The valley has one of America's best sets of cross-country ski trails.

THE SKIING—ATTITASH

Attitash closed a few years ago—a few bad winters in a row and stiff competition from other areas dealt the small mountain what might have seemed a death blow. But it reopened shortly thereafter with some of the newest and most modern snowmaking equipment in the East. Combine the snowmaking coverage (sixteen of twenty trails), a limited lift-ticket sales policy, and a nicely designed mountain, and it's clear that Attitash has made impressive use of relatively scant resources.

Most of the slopes at Attitash are great for intermediates, though experts will be challenged by the steepness of Tightrope and the often enormous moguls on Idiot's Option. The top of the mountain can become quite congested, because Northwest Passage has no snowmaking and is often closed. The broad runs on the western side of the mountain are great for novice skiers working their way up to intermediate level.

Because the management limits lift-ticket sales, lines are rarely longer than fifteen minutes on weekends and negligible on weekdays.

THE SKIING—WILDCAT

While Attitash limits its ticket sales, Wildcat doesn't, and the result is predictable—on weekends, the place is jammed, with forty-five minute waits at the little two-person gondola not uncommon.

But even with these odds, the skiing at Wildcat is a good deal more

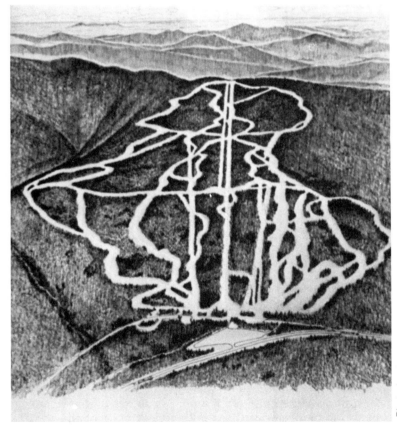

Photo by Joan Eaton

challenging. First of all, the mountain is much larger than Attitash (2,100 vertical feet at Wildcat versus 1,500 at Attitash). Secondly, Wildcat's snowmaking system is not as extensive, and the weather at Wildcat can be ferocious. The Forest Service folks at Mount Washington, just across the street from the ski area, proudly declare that the peak enjoys the "world's worst weather." The highest wind ever measured—231 miles per hour—was recorded at the summit of Mount Washington.

There are some fine long runs at Wildcat suitable for skiers at almost any level. Polecat, a novice/lower intermediate trail, runs almost three miles from summit to base, covered by snowmaking the whole way. Lynx and Lower Catapult will be the experts' choices. Intermediates can ski most of the mountain—on days with good snow, the expert runs are challenging but not impossible, and on icy, windy days, the novice runs become a lot tougher.

THE TOWN/NIGHTLIFE

The motels glare, the restaurants beckon, and you're faced with a barrage of decisions. But you'll have plenty of time to consider your options, because chances are good that you'll be stuck in a traffic jam on Route 16, the main road through town. Welcome to North Conway.

North Conway, in the middle of peaceful New Hampshire, is probably where you'll want to stay. You'll find cheap motels, quick food, and nightlife. For a friendly bar and the largest french fries you've ever seen, go to Horsefeathers in the center of town. Merlino's serves good steak and Italian dishes. At Barnaby's and the Up Country Saloon you'll get decent food and live music. While Barnaby's tends to be more popular with an over-thirty crowd, the Up Country caters to the under-thirty rockers. Tin Pan Alley and Le Bistrot are quiet, good restaurants with charming, turn-of-the-century atmosphere. The Bernerhof is acknowledged as the best restaurant in town for its fine European cuisine, while the Scottish Lion, a good deal cheaper, also gets fine reviews.

But probably the most popular place to eat and then hang out for a few hours is the Red Parka Pub, a few miles north of town. The restaurant serves great ribs and every Monday there's a buffet. Have free popcorn while you enjoy the camaraderie in the pub. This is not a wild rock 'n' roll spot by any means (you're in New Hampshire, remember), but it is a perfect place to have dinner and then retire to the pub for a round or three of drinks.

LODGING

The best way to get assistance in choosing among the numerous accommodations available in North Conway is to contact the local 13

Chamber of Commerce (603–356–3171). We will tell you about some of the best bets.

If you want to be near Attitash, try the Attitash Mountain Village, directly across the street from the mountain. The motel units and condos are comfortable, and it has a good restaurant, lounge, and swimming pool. Prices are anywhere from $40 to $150, and some great package deals are available. Down the road in Bartlett, the Sky Valley Motel has a similar range of choices, from motel units to chalets, and prices start at $33 and go to $85. The elegant Dana Place Inn is the nearest lodge to Wildcat and includes bed and breakfast in its highly praised dining room. The Eagle Mountain House in Jackson is another fine choice. A sprawling old resort that is being lovingly refurbished, it has excellent dining. Across the street from the Jackson Ski Touring Foundation, the Eagle Mountain House is very popular with college students and runs from $40 to $60. Every Sunday night, artists in a renowned concert series perform in the lobby.

In town, you will find everything from quaint inns to impersonal motels. You could stay at the 1785 Inn, one of the oldest houses in the valley. It's a lovely bed-and-breakfast that costs $35 to $55 per night. Another nice old home, The Old Red Inn, also has cottages, and the Cranmore Mountain Lodge has a barn loft and a dorm (both in the $20 to $50 range).

You will find that there isn't much difference among the dozens of motels to choose from. The Arends Motel, the Briarcliff Motel, the Crestwood Motor Lodge, the Green Granite Motel, and, of course, the famous Presidential Waterbed Motel (which presidents stayed there, we wonder) all offer rooms in the $20 to $50 range, and most have color cable TV, among other things. Again, call the Chamber of Commerce and compare prices.

TWO ADDITIONAL POINTS

There are a couple of other points you may find helpful on your trip to Washington Valley.

First, the Jackson Ski Touring Foundation is regarded by many as the premier cross-country ski center in America, if not the world. It offers miles and miles of trails through the pristine forests of the White Mountains, and you could take the gondola to the peak of Wildcat and ski down the thirteen-mile trail to Jackson. Many people in the valley avoid downhill skiing and devote themselves to the cross-country trails.

Second, skiers who like to shop for bargains (and we hope that includes all the readers of this book) may have a tough choice—there are so many discount factory outlets in North Conway that the ski slopes may begin to seem like an expensive diversion. You can buy everything from Scandinavian kitchenware to Hathaway shirts to Converse shoes to camping gear at 30 to 50 percent off retail, sometimes more. Though the stores are far from elegant and the sales help is minimal, the discounts more than make up for these slight inconveniences.

ACCESSIBILITY

North Conway is about a three-hour drive from Boston, seven from New York. By air, it's best to fly to Boston and rent a car, but Portland, Maine and Manchester, New Hampshire also have airports. Trailways has bus service to North Conway.

LISTINGS

Attitash Mountain
Route 302
Bartlett, NH   03812
603-374-2369 or toll-free 800-258-0316
Lodging: 603-374-2386

Wildcat Mountain
Route 16
Pinkham Notch
Jackson, NH   03846
603-466-3326

Jackson Ski Touring Foundation
Route 16B
Jackson, NH   03846
603-383-9355

Mount Washington Valley Chamber of Commerce
P.O. Box 385
Mount Washington Valley, NH   03860
603-356-3171

LIFT TICKET

Attitash: midweek $16, weekend $19
Wildcat: Sunday-Friday $15, Saturdays and holidays $18; two-for-one
    ($17) on Wednesday, plus $2 for gondola pass.

RESTAURANTS AND BARS

Horsefeathers, Route 16, 356-2687.
Merlino's, Route 16, 356-9705.
Barnaby's, Route 16, 356-5781.
The Up Country Saloon, Route 16, 356-9782.
Tin Pan Alley, Kearsarge Street, 356-3922.
Le Bistrot, Kearsarge Street, 356-5295.
The Bernerhof, Route 302, Glen, 383-4414.

The Scottish Lion, Route 16, 356-6381.

Red Parka Pub, Route 302, Glen, 383-4344.

LODGING

Attitash Mountain Village, Route 302, Bartlett, 374-2386.

Sky Valley Motel, Route 302, Bartlett, 374-2322.

Dana Place Inn, Route 16, Jackson, 383-6822.

Eagle Mountain House, Carter Notch Road, Jackson, 383-4347.

The 1785 Inn, Route 16, 356-9025.

The Old Red Inn, Route 16, 356-2642.

Cranmore Mountain Lodge, Kearsarge Road, 356-2044.

Arends Motel, Route 16, 356-2976.

Briarcliff Motel, Route 16, 356-5584.

Crestwood Motor Lodge, Route 16, 356-5492.

Green Granite Motel, Route 16, 356-3960.

Presidential Waterbed Motel, Route 16, 356-9744.

WATERVILLE VALLEY AND LOON MOUNTAIN

With no disrespect intended, Waterville Valley's best selling point is its location: just over two hours from Boston on I-93. This is not to discount the friendly atmosphere, solid intermediate trails, reasonable prices, and not unreasonable lift lines. Its easy access, well-designed trails, and scenic beauty all share in making it a popular mountain. And just up the road, Loon Mountain is developing into more than just a place to handle Waterville's overflow.

Despite its rather glamorous reputation (the Kennedys ski here), Waterville is primarily a day area for skiers from Boston and the surrounding region. Since so many skiers head for home after skiing, there are very few restaurants and nightspots. There aren't even many hotels. Those skiers who do stay overnight usually stay in a condominium, as nearly all of the lodging consists of condos. Most inns have been converted into time-sharing units. The village itself has a permanent population of only 199. There are few places to stay, and little to do.

You will find this a rather short chapter, because although Waterville is New Hampshire's premier ski area, there is little to discuss. If you're coming up for the day or planning to buy a condo, Waterville is a great place. But if you're planning a ski week, you may do well to look elsewhere.

THE SKIING

The White Peak chair is the major lift for the mountain. Lines can reach twenty-five minutes on weekends, but they never get much longer, because Waterville limits the lift-ticket sales. The chair provides access to intermediate and expert runs (many of which are frequently closed). Intermediates will enjoy trails like Tippecanoe or And Tyler Too, while experts can try Sel's Choice, Utter Abandon, or the runs under the chair. True Grit and Lower Bobby's Run are the most challenging runs, but if they're open, the lines at the Sunnyside chair will be much shorter. At the top of the mountain, the short High Country trail opens up three more expert slopes, plus the Glade, also

WATERVILLE VALLEY, NEW HAMPSHIRE

rated expert. Intermediates can avoid the long base lines by skiing the North Side chair.

Less accomplished intermediates will like the wide-open, gentle trails of Valley Run and Rock Island, served by a double and triple chair. Beginners can learn on the Lower Meadows double chairlift, or the Pasture J-bar. Finally, the little-used Snow's Mountain Ski Area is across the street from the main mountain. It has a chair and several intermediate trails.

THE TOWN/NIGHTLIFE

Nightlife may mean the drive back to Boston. If you're staying, go to the Fourways for the rock 'n' roll bands in its conference-center complex. The Scandinavi-Inn also has bands at times, as does the Valley Inn and Tavern. None of these places is a thrill. The William Tell Bar, a drinking spot and restaurant, is the liveliest spot.

The list of restaurants is short. In the village, the Fourways is the best spot, with the Valley Inn and Tavern other possible choices. The Finish Line, at Snow's Mountain, has a lot more atmosphere and serves interesting food. William Tell's has good Swiss cuisine at reasonable prices.

LODGING

Lodging consists mainly of condos, which are all a shuttle ride away from the slopes. The nicest units are probably at the Mad River ($285 for two bedrooms for a weekend), and among the least expensive are the Windsor Hill units. Windsor Hill costs $160 for one bedroom for a weekend. The Tri-Pyramid condos, also among the nicest, cost $200 for a weekend for one bedroom. They have access to a fully equipped health spa.

Many of the hotels in Waterville Valley have become time-sharing establishments. The Valley Inn and Tavern is an attractive complex costing $130 per person for a weekend, meals included. The Snowy Owl Inn will cost about $70 a night for a double. Both are immaculate. Farther down the road is the Scandinavi-Inn, an unpretentious establishment that serves meals.

LOON MOUNTAIN

About ten miles north of Waterville, Loon is a relatively new resort, used principally as an overflow area for Waterville Valley. Recently a number of homes and condos have been built, and Loon is developing its own following—calling itself "New England's fastest growing ski area." Like Waterville, Loon has no enticing nightlife to lure you from the drive home. The skiing is mainly advanced beginner and intermediate, and the lines are generally shorter than at Waterville. Loon also has a limited lift-ticket sales policy.

Loon is a nice place, but it exists in Waterville's shadow. Although the skiing is nice, we suggest that if Waterville is too crowded, you head up the road a few miles to Cannon Mountain in Franconia, where the slopes are more challenging.

ACCESSIBILITY

Both Waterville Valley and Loon are right off I-93, about two and a half hours from Boston and six and a half from New York. Manchester has an airport, though flying into Boston and renting a car might be easier.

LISTINGS

Waterville Valley Ski Resort
Waterville Valley, NH   03223
603–236–8311

LODGING

In New Hampshire, call toll-free 800–552–4767
Outside New Hampshire, call 800–258–8988

Loon Mountain
Kancamagus Highway
Lincoln, NH   03251
603–745–8111
Lodging: 603–745–2244

LIFT TICKET

$16 weekdays, $20 weekdays and holidays.

LIFT TICKET

$17 ($3 surcharge for gondola on weekends and holidays)

RESTAURANTS

William Tell Restaurant, Route 49, 726–3618.
Village Inn and Tavern, Tecumseh Road, 236–8336.
Finish Line, at Snow's Mountain, 236–8800.
Scandinavi-Inn, Route 49, Campton, 726–3737.

LODGING

(*For condos or hotels, contact Waterville Valley.*)
Village Inn and Tavern, Waterville Valley, 236–8336.
Snowy Owl Inn, Waterville Valley, 236–8383.
Scandinavi-Inn, Route 49, Campton, 726–3737.

BROMLEY

Since Fred Pabst, the beer magnate, started Bromley in 1937, it's been a family ski area, but in all that time the area has remained in Stratton's shadow—it's the smaller, less flashy, and less expensive of the two resorts.

Over the years, Bromley has developed a large cadre of devoted skiers for several good reasons. The area frequently boasts the best snow in southern Vermont, due to equipment and exposure. Pabst invested in snowmaking equipment before most areas knew the machines even existed, and Bromley's southern exposure makes for great suntans; more importantly, it melts the hardpack snow by noon. So even if Stratton's snow is deeper, Bromley's snow may well be in better shape.

Traditionally, skiers went to Bromley for the family atmosphere. The lines were shorter, the prices lower, and the atmosphere friendlier than at Stratton. A long line at Bromley, for example, means fifteen minutes, while one at Stratton can last forty-five minutes to an hour. The area advertised less, so it attracted fewer buses and ski commandos from New York City.

Unfortunately, Fred Pabst sold Bromley, which then lost much of its unspoiled appeal. Though the trails bear the same Pabst names— Blue Ribbon, Pabst Peril—gone is the old traditional atmosphere. Not only did the new owners advertise heavily, they also built a huge condo complex next to the slopes. Locals still ski Bromley, but now they're outnumbered by out-of-state visitors. To make matters worse, the new owners sold Bromley to Stratton, which jacked up the prices.

THE SKIING

But no matter who owns Bromley, they can't take away the sun, the shorter lines, or the well-planned slopes. Bromley has three major and two minor double chairlifts, plus a J-bar. Although Bromley rarely challenges the expert, the East Side can appeal to the good skier. The chairlift serves expert trails that are tougher than Stratton's. And the wait at the East Side lift is always short—five minutes in the morning, and fifteen minutes at most in the afternoon. From the East Side you can also cut over to the West Side, ski an intermediate trail, and then shoot back to the East Side on trails like East Meadow. That way you can avoid the lift lines.

On the West Side, Thruway offers long, wide-open skiing while Shin-Cracker and Blazer cut narrow paths through the woods. All the trails funnel down to only two areas, so no cross-country tramping is ever required. But mogul lovers won't like Bromley: the resort bulldozes its bumps every night.

Bromley is best skied on weekends and during March. If the snow lasts, the resort can't be beat for spring skiing. Thanks to the southern exposure, the sun melts the snow and browns the body.

THE TOWN/NIGHTLIFE

As we said, Bromley is a family place. So there isn't much nightlife. All nightlife is a drive away and usually isn't worth the trip. Alfie's is a disco housed in a round barn and is hard to take seriously. In Londonderry, The Mill, a favorite with the locals, has rock 'n' roll bands in a hand-hewn barn. But for any real nightlife, go to Stratton (see the Stratton chapter for details).

For cross-country skiing, avoid Stratton's center—it's a golf course—and visit Viking Ski Touring Center in Londonderry or Wild Wings in Peru. Viking is by far the larger center, but Wild Wings has trails in some wonderful woods. Stop by the town of Peru and visit the general store. Manchester is worth the trip just to walk on the marble sidewalks and to visit the mansions like Hildene. Finally, if the huge Equinox House really is restored as planned, try to reserve a room in this wonderful, once-glorious hotel.

RESTAURANTS

Manchester has some great restaurants. The Three Clock Inn and the Toll Gate Lodge shouldn't be missed, nor should The Reluctant Panther. The Nordic Inn serves its delicious cuisine to outsiders, too. The Village Auberge is a quality French establishment.

For more typical ski fare—steak and seafood—Haig's and The Red Fox Inn make it worth the trip to Stratton. The most popular dining establishment is the now-franchised Sirloin Saloon, which has reasonably priced food and a great salad bar. For the budget-conscious, the Double Hex or Garlic John's are the places to try.

LODGING

Manchester is well known for its lovely inns and exceptional restaurants. But again, all the inns and the restaurants except one are a drive away. There is no cluster of development surrounding Bromley's base, except for the condos. The Bromley Sun Lodge sits perched like a garage next to the slopes. A two-day weekend with meals costs $110.

The Nordic Inn, five minutes from Bromley, has its own superb dining facilities, individually decorated rooms, and miles of cross-country skiing trails. It's worth the $125 to $139 price for a weekend.

Another sophisticated inn lies about twenty minutes away in Manchester. The Reluctant Panther has superb food but, unfortunately, meals are extra. A weekend costs $47 to $75. Other country inns include The Inn at Manchester, and the 1811 House.

Just a quarter mile from Bromley is Johnny Seesaw's, a traditional ski lodge that also has cottages. A weekend costs $88 to $116, with meals. A mile down the road in the other direction is the modern Kandahar Lodge.

For those on a tight budget, the Skylight Ski Lodge costs just $54 for a weekend, bunk beds and meals included.

A bit further from Bromley are the typical motels. The 1878 Carriage House, Aspen Inn, and the Snowbound Motel (which also has chalets) are two of the closer ones; rooms cost about $35.

Finally, Bromley has a large and thriving condo community next door. Many of the units have spectacular views, and all are within skiing or walking distance. Contact the Bromley office for reservations.

ACCESSIBILITY

Same as Stratton.

LISTINGS

Bromley Mountain
P.O. Box 1130
Manchester Center, VT   05255
802-824-5522
Reservations: 802-824-6915

NIGHTLIFE

Alfie's, Route 11, Manchester Center, 362-2637.
The Mill, Route 11, Londonderry, 824-3247.

RESTAURANTS

Double Hex, Routes 11 and 30, Manchester Depot, 362-1270.
Garlic John's, Routes 11 and 30, Manchester Center, 362-9843.
Haig's, Route 30, Stratton, 297-1300.
Nordic Inn, Route 11, Landgrove, 824-6444.
Red Fox Inn, Winhall Hollow Road, Bondville, 297-2543.
Reluctant Panther, West Road, Manchester Village, 362-2568.
Sirloin Saloon, Routes 11 and 30, 362-2600.
Three Clock Inn, South Londonderry, 824-6327.

Toll Gate Lodge, Routes 11 and 30, 362-1779.
Village Auberge, Route 30, Dorset, 867-5715.

LODGING

1811 House, Box 207, Manchester, 362-1811.
Inn at Manchester, Box 356, Manchester, 362-1793.
Nordic Inn, Box 96, Londonderry, 824-6444.
Reluctant Panther Inn, Box 678, Manchester, 362-2568.
Aspen Motel, Box 548, Manchester Center, 362-2450.
1878 Carriage House Motel, Route 7, 362-1706.
Snow Bound Motel, Route 7, Manchester Center, 362-2145.
Bromley Sun Lodge, Route 11, Peru, 824-6400.
Johnny Seesaw's, Box 68, Peru, 824-5533.
Kandahar Lodge, Routes 11 and 30, Manchester, 824-5531.
Skylight Ski Lodge, Routes 11 and 30, Manchester Center, 362-2566.

JAY PEAK

Just four and a half hours from Boston there is a quiet, relaxed ski experience largely undiscovered by U.S. skiers. At Jay Peak, you'll find some of Vermont's steepest trails, longest runs, best snow, coldest weather, and shortest lift lines. It's lent an international flavor by the Canadian families and day skiers who come over from Montreal. It was originally hoped Jay Peak would bring economic growth to the region, but the resort has never gained the size or style that was originally planned. Perhaps the mountain is a bit too far away—and too cold—to draw the New York or Boston crowds. Although it doesn't hum at night, there are some places to drink or dance. But most people simply eat dinner at the lodge and go off to sleep so they'll be ready for another day of short lines and good, inexpensive skiing.

Coupled with increasing snowmaking abilities and an average annual snowfall of 275 inches, peak-to-base skiing from early November through April and sometimes even into May is nearly assured. With the largest ski lift in Vermont—a sixty-passenger aerial tramway—you'll find access to novice, intermediate, and expert trails.

THE SKIING

Two mountains, Big Jay and Little Jay, are serviced by six chairlifts, two T-bars, and a tram. Thirty trails run down the nearly 4,000-foot peaks, which have a vertical drop of 2,100 feet. Top-to-bottom runs are available to skiers of all abilities. You can ride the tram to the summit and find trails leading back to the Base Lodge Tram or the Red Chair. However, Jay's trails tend to wander more than most, with steep and flat sections common on all trails. The lines stay short on the weekdays, but on weekends, Montrealers deluge the place.

Little Jay is home to a 3,600-foot T-bar and the most challenging trails. The U.N. trail was ranked the fourth toughest in America, thanks to its consistently steep pitch. Many of the expert trails run from top to bottom.

There is ample terrain as well for novices. While two lower T-bars deliver you to nice practice slopes, the more adventuresome novice can ride the tram to the top.

THE TOWN/NIGHTLIFE

Jay is usually pretty peaceful at night, except when the college kids invade during ski weeks. If your tastes run to a hard-drinking ski- 25 patrol bar, then head for the Belfry. The Thirsty Boot at Granny Grunt's dormitory and Corky's have dancing. Corky's, however, has live bands. College students make up most of the crowd. Plan on burning off most of your energy on the slopes.

RESTAURANTS

The Hotel Jay, at the base of the peak, and the Black Lantern Inn in Montgomery Center serve excellent gourmet cuisine in a warm and cozy setting. The Hotel Jay's menu is more extensive, but nonguests will have to pay more. Both serve hearty breakfasts, too. The Jay Village Inn has a varied menu, but guests on the Modified American Plan are limited to two of the less expensive menu items. For standard fare at standard prices there's the Inglenook. Pleasures offers specialty sandwiches and quiche for $3 to $5, while the Belfry is known for reasonably priced steaks, burgers, and seafood. For seafood alone, try Wayne's Fisherman Platter in Newport.

LODGING

The most convenient, luxurious and expensive ($70 for a single, $120 for a double) accommodations are found in the Hotel Jay. Nearby, the Snowline combines lodge atmosphere with a motel. Breakfasts are included in the price of $36 for a double. The Inglenook Lodge has the area's only indoor swimming pool, plus racquetball courts and a sauna. A double, including meals, costs $80. Casual and comfortable, it has a sunken lounge and circular fireplace.

The Schneehutte provides bed, breakfast, and family-style dinners in a dormitory setting at economy rates ($20). Granny Grunt's does the same, and, as we mentioned, has an adjoining nightspot. Due to the barely adequate guestrooms and the limited dining available, the Jay Village Inn is best avoided. The Black Lantern Inn, built as a stagecoach stop in 1803, is eight miles from Jay Peak. Drive over country roads to reach this romantic inn. The gourmet food and charming atmosphere make it well worth the $72 for a double, which includes meals.

You can obtain information about the few available condominium units through the Lodging Association. Alpine Haven, in nearby Montgomery Center, provides a private, rustic setting for eighty-two chalets, each with a fireplace and two to six bedrooms.

If you can withstand the cold temperatures, you might want to call ahead and barter for January—it's a slow month. For example, the Hotel Jay's "college week" package for the first three weeks in January costs $199, and includes five days of meals, lodging, and lift tickets.

A great hint from some of the Canadians: the ski area takes Canadian money at a par with U.S. dollars. Since Jay is just eight miles from the Canadian border, it will be worth anyone's while to exchange money before skiing.

ACCESSIBILITY

Jay Peak is five hours from Boston, seven from New York, and two from Montreal. The nearest airport is in Burlington, Vermont, about an hour away, and Jay runs a van from the airport for $7. Amtrak serves Burlington and St. Alban's. Greyhound (via Vermont Transit) serves Newport.

LISTINGS

Jay Peak Ski Area
Route 242
Jay, VT   05859
802-988-2611

LIFT TICKET

$21

RESTAURANTS AND BARS

Hotel Jay, Jay Peak, 988-2611.
Inglenook, Upper Mountain Road, Route 242, 988-2880.
Jay Village Inn, Route 242, 988-2643.
Black Lantern Inn, Route 118, Montgomery, 326-4507.
Snowline Pub, Route 242, 988-2822.
The Belfry, Route 242, Montgomery Center, 326-4400.
Pleasures, Route 242, 988-4368.
Wayne's Fisherman Platter, Newport Center Road, Newport, 334-7763.
Thirsty Boot, Route 118, Montgomery, no phone.
Corky's, Route 118, Montgomery, no phone.

LODGING

Hotel Jay, Jay Peak, 988-2611.
Inglenook Lodge, Upper Mountain Road, Route 242, 988-2880.
Jay Village Inn, Route 242, 988-2643.
Schneehutte, Route 242, 988-4020.
Black Lantern Inn, Route 118, Montgomery, 326-4507.
Snowline Lodge, Route 242, 988-2822.
Alpine Haven Chalets, Route 242, Montgomery Center, 326-4567.
Granny Grunt's, Route 118, Montgomery, 326-4740.

KILLINGTON

Killington is the eastern ski area of extremes: it's the largest resort, gets the most natural snow in the east, and makes the most snow in the world. It opens earliest and closes latest, and has the most lifts, the most skiers, and the most lodging. This is not cozy, intimate, rugged New England skiing. Killington is an industry, a mass-participation, high-volume business, and you'll develop an extreme reaction: you'll either love it or hate it.

Killington is one of the few true destination resorts in the east, an area that Joe Smith from Atlanta might consider for a one-week ski vacation with the wife and kids. Though Killington's main crowd is from New York and Massachusetts, it also competes with Vail, Aspen, Mammoth, and other major resorts for nationwide attention. Although the numerous package deals, group rates, and special events are designed to lure out-of-state skiers, the eastern skier also benefits. Ski instruction is top-notch, and "customer assistance" is excellent.

Constructed of six interconnected mountains, Killington can be skied for a full weekend and you'll never see the same trail twice, although it's common to be disoriented by the numerous trails and lifts. Unfortunately Killington's trail map is as large as a tablecloth, so many skiers just ask for directions. If Vail can put its mountain, the Back Bowls, *and* Beaver Creek on one convenient piece of paper, anyone can.

So the size of Killington has its obvious pros and cons: the diversity of trails is wonderful and the mountains are a joy, but there are drawbacks—heavy traffic in the morning and afternoon, and you'll have to resign yourself to substantial waits for some lifts and meals.

THE SKIING

It's hard to know where to begin, so we'll try to be orderly, and work our way west to east:

Sunrise Mountain. Two long and rather boring novice trails wind down Sunrise Mountain—Sun Dog, which has snowmaking, and Juggernaut, which doesn't. There are two brief expert runs and a mid-length intermediate trail, but for the most part this is a beginner's area. If you're a day skier, try parking at Sunrise's base.

Bear Mountain. This is where the experts stay. Some mogul fiends will park at Bear's base and ride the quad and triple lifts all day so they can ski Outer Limits—the steepest run in the East, with a relent-

KILLINGTON, VERMONT

less series of macho moguls. Devil's Fiddle, on the eastern side, is less steep and tends to get icier. The third run on the mountain, Wildfire, is a blast for advanced intermediates who want to work on their bump technique.

Skye Peak. Calling Skye Peak a distinctly different mountain is kind of fudging it, since it's really just a bump coming down from Killington Peak. But it does have a gondola midstation, and Superstar is a very tough expert run to the main base area.

Killington Peak. Highest of the six mountains at 4,241 feet, Killington Peak is the terminus for the gondola, the longest ski lift in the U.S. (3.5 miles— a twenty-five minute ride). A full range of trails is available: the peaceful Juggernaut and Solitude; the fun Four-Mile Trail, which becomes intermediate halfway down; The Jug and Rime, two demanding intermediate runs; and Big Dipper and Cascade, trails which gave Killington early credibility with experts.

Snowdon Mountain. This is probably the most popular area at Killington. All Snowdon Mountain's trails have snowmaking, and the capacity of its two lifts is impressive. While lift lines are rarely longer than fifteen minutes, the slopes get packed, especially with experimenting novices who are trying their first "real" trails after skiing the Snowshed slopes. Hence, the Bunny Buster trail is aptly named. Chute is a fun blue run, too, but intermediates should venture onto 29 the black Conclusion and Interceptor—they're not impossibly steep, and they're good trails on which to develop new skills.

Rams Head Mountain. Although it is often the least crowded area at Killington, Rams Head has few trails. Timberline and Swirl are good warm-up trails for the first runs in the morning, while Header is a bit more than a warm-up.

THE TOWN/NIGHTLIFE

The only real town is Rutland, eleven miles to the east. Most lodging and nightlife at Killington is on the four-mile access road from Route 4—basically a long row of condos and lodges, with a few restaurants and shops.

Most of the lodges and inns have small restaurants and bars, and since many skiers come on a Modified American Plan (MAP)—breakfast and dinner included in the room price—many people simply return to their lodge, have a drink, dine, and retire.

But if you're a single, there are a few nightspots that cater to you.

Late afternoon happy hours at the Kings Four and the Red Rob Inn are very popular with locals and skiers. Both have live music, and the atmosphere varies from cozy to raucous, depending on the crowd. Don't miss the famous Goombay Smash served in a Mason jar at the Red Rob.

Mother Shapiro's, run by a guy who likes to think he's the stereotypical Jewish mother, is a small but very friendly bar that serves hot sandwiches and excellent soups. The bar at Charity's is rustic, and the attractive restaurant has steak and burgers. It's a bit expensive. You'll find a good $3 buffet during Happy Hour at Nightspot in the Killington Mall. On weekends it attracts the New York disco crowd. It's a little too disco for our tastes, though.

If it's rock 'n' roll you want, head for the Pickle Barrel. With live bands, a large dance area, lots of specials, and a charming maze of floors and stairs and balconies, it's easily the best nightclub in the area. The Pickle Barrel attracts a casual group of locals and nonchic skiers.

The prime rib is excellent at the Wobbly Barn, a Killington institution, and the large bar has live music, but it's getting rather expensive. Actually, you could fill up at the large soup, salad, and bread bar for $5.95. Including drinks, though, you'll be lucky to escape for less than $17.

With a neat, funky, slightly sixties atmosphere, the Back Home Cafe in Rutland serves good homemade food and Italian dishes, and has an excellent bakery. For really fine Italian cuisine go to the Casa Blanca. The 1787 Governor's Table, offering a continental menu, is an elegant and romantic spot with candlelight and surprisingly low prices.

Most of the other Killington restaurants are the standard, ski-area, steak-and-seafood spots with $20 price tags. You can get an inexpensive breakfast at The Coffee Shop, an old-fashioned diner on Route 4 near the access road.

LODGING

You can choose from over one hundred lodges, motels, and condos, each with two dozen deals—two-day, five-day, and seven-day packages, European Plans (no meals), Modified American Plans (breakfast and dinner), lessons, rental equipment, lift tickets, and on and on. As with the other major ski resorts, check with the Killington lodging bureau. You should also look at the lodging directory Killington publishes—probably the most comprehensive and helpful guide published by any U.S. ski area. It lists prices, locations, and complete deals, and it's fairly simple to use. However, we will give you a basic idea.

The farther down the access road you go, the less expensive lodging will be, especially by the time you reach Rutland, Pittsfield, and Woodstock. You may prefer the convenience of being near a shuttle bus stop on Killington Road, but if a fifteen- to thirty-minute drive isn't too inconvenient, try some of these, all within the $15 to $28 range. To the north, there's the Fleur de Lis Lodge, the Swiss Farm Lodge, and the Colton Guest Farm. To the east, check out the Sherburne Valley Inn, the Turn of River Lodge, and the Ottauquechee Motel. Toward Rutland, try the Journey's End Motor Inn, the White Stone Motel, and the Mendon Mountain Orchards and Motel.

Of the half-dozen condominiums at the base of the mountain, the Trail Creek and Mountain Green Condos are the most convenient. The Villager at Killington offers the closest lodging to the slopes and all the amenities you could want. The above are in the $50 to $100 range, and higher.

One nice thing about the lodges along the access road is that most offer dormitory accomodations as well as normal rooms. The Alpenhof, the Chalet Killington, the Fractured Rooster, and the Killington Fireside Lodge all have dorm space for $15 to $30 or so. The Snowed Inn, the Skol Haus, the Chalet International, and the Chalet Roedig, all in the $20 to $35 range per night, are also quite popular among the budget-minded.

ACCESSIBILITY

Killington is 11 miles east of Rutland, and 14 miles west of Woodstock. New York is about 250 miles south, Boston 160 miles east. The small airport in Rutland is serviced by Precision Airlines. Both Precision and Command Airways fly into Lebanon, New Hampshire, an hour away. Amtrak has service to White River Junction, Vermont. ARK Transportation runs a shuttle bus from both airports and the train station. Greyhound/Vermont Transit has bus service directly to Killington through Rutland. Along the access road, a shuttle bus stops at the major restaurants and the condo units near the base.

LISTINGS

Killington Ski Resort
Killington, VT 05751
802–422–3333
Lodging: 802–422–3711

LIFT TICKET

$24 weekdays, $25 weekends and holidays

RESTAURANTS AND BARS

Along Killington Road:
The Kings Four, 422–3594.
The Red Rob Inn, 422–3303.
Mother Shapiro's, 422–9933.
Charity's, 422-3800.
Nightspot, 422–9885.
The Pickle Barrel, 422–3035.
The Wobbly Barn, 422–3392.

In Rutland:
Back Home Cafe, Center Street, 775–2104.
Casa Blanca, Grove Street, 773–7401.
1787 Governor's Table, Main Street, 775–7277.

Near the junction of Routes 4 and 100:
The Coffee Shop, 775–4840.

LODGING

Fleur de Lis Lodge, Route 100 North, Pittsfield, 746–8943.
Swiss Farm Lodge, Route 100 North, Pittsfield, 746–8341.
Colton Guest Farm, Route 100 North, Pittsfield, 746–8901.
Sherburne Valley Inn, Route 4 East, 422–9888.
Turn of River Lodge, Route 4 East, 422–3766.
Ottauquechee Motel, Route 4 East, Woodstock, 672–3404.
Journey's End Motor Inn, Route 4 West, Mendon, 773–6644.
White Stone Motel, Route 4 West, Mendon, 773–2155.
Mendon Mountain Orchards and Motel, Route 4 West, Mendon, 775–5477.
Trail Creek Condominiums, 101 Killington Road, 422–3101.
Mountain Green Condominiums, 101 Killington Road, 422–3101.
The Villager at Killington, 101 Killington Road, 422–3101.

The Alpenhof, Killington Road, 422-9787.
The Chalet Killington, Killington Road, 422-3451.
The Fractured Rooster, Telefon Trail Road, 422-3288.
Killington Fireside Lodge, Killington Road, 422-3361.
The Snowed Inn, Killington Road, 422-3407.
The Skol Haus, Killington Road, 422-3305.
The Chalet International, Killington Road, 422-3481.
The Chalet Roedig, Killington Road, 422-3810.

MAD RIVER

Mad River is among the few eastern ski areas that have retained their old-fashioned New England charm. While many eastern ski areas seem like another stop on the Lexington Avenue subway, Mad River is a refreshing change. And even better, it has some of the most challenging and imaginative trails in the East; trails like Chute and Fall Line, served by the old single chair, equal anything at Stowe or Killington.

Mad River will entertain either the single skier or the family. Its nearness to Sugarbush, a singles mecca, ensures great nightlife. And the limited number of skiers who come to Mad River are devoted. It's the type of place where skiwear means blue jeans and a CB jacket, and upper class means a senior in college. Most of the people at the lodge seem to know (and like) each other. It's easy for families to ski at Mad River, since three of the four lifts converge.

As the ski area has been trying to increase its midweek crowd, the local innkeepers have joined forces to make Mad River a bargain. For example, at a nearby condo complex, five days of skiing and lodging for students runs just $129, while other inns include breakfast and dinner for as little as $155.

THE SKIING

Mad River has long been known as the *expert's* mountain. But the management is quick to point out that, in addition to the great expert trails, the area is well supplied with a range of novice and intermediate terrains. The true beginner, however, will still feel left out. When the snow is good, a beginner can manage, but when it gets icy he could be in for trouble.

Mad River is famous for its single chair and two of the expert trails that run off it, Chute and Fall Line. Chute runs straight under the chair, accumulating a good supply of moguls. One skier (known as the Chutist) flies up from Washington, D.C., nearly every weekend and just skis the Chute all day. A word of warning: the intermediate trail from the top would be marked expert almost anywhere else. But intermediates can get off the chair halfway and ski down comfortably.

The Birdland chair is suitable for novices. Located halfway up the mountain, it climbs just 500 feet in its 2,400-foot length. Take the Sunnyside chair to the Fox and Vixen trails and then connect to the Snail trail, which reaches Birdland.

Intermediates can select among the trails off the Sunnyside chair, and will find that expert runs, such as Panther or Partridge, are not terribly intimidating.

At most, lift lines on the two main chairs will be twenty minutes on weekends. Since Mad River doesn't have the snowmaking capability of most Vermont areas, if it seems like a weekend where that's essential, go elsewhere. You will also find that Mad River doesn't have the grooming abilities found elsewhere—for example, it lets moguls build up. But just because conditions don't sound perfect, don't be put off—it's just that Mad River may be more honest about its slopes than other resorts.

THE TOWN/NIGHTLIFE

Routes 17 and 100 are lined with restaurants, lodges, and nightspots. The Mad River Barn often gets the afternoon crowd and ski patrol and ski instructors coming off the trails. Moose Lips and Gallagher's are right across the street from each other. Both are dance and beer-guzzling establishments. Moose Lips leans toward country, while Gallagher's plays more rock 'n' roll and reggae. The Blue Tooth, on the road to Sugarbush, gets the college and high school kids with its rock 'n' roll. Michel's and Chez Henri, both of which also serve dinner, are upscale places.

RESTAURANTS

You can get anything from potato skins to eggplant parmigiana at Moose Lips, where entrees run from $5 to $12. Gallagher's has similar fare. For excellent French food, dine at The Common Man, which is housed in a barn. Dinner costs between $8 and $11. A popular soup-and-sandwich place, Beggar's Banquet, runs $3 to $8. Another fine French spot in the same price bracket is Sam Rupert's. Have delicious Chinese food in the $6 to $10 range at the China Barn. For a good French meal and dancing, visit Michel's or Chez Henri. In the Sugarbush complex itself, try Odyssey for pizza and Phoenix for fine dinners and gourmet desserts. Wake up at Reveille, a restaurant at Sergeant Pepper's, famous for breakfast. Some of the lodges, such as Tucker Hill and the Waitsfield Inn, also serve nonguests.

LODGING

Mad River doesn't have the usual New England maze of condominiums. The few trailside houses and condos are rented through Mad River itself; prices are set by the homeowners.

Lodging listed under this section is closer to Mad River than Sugarbush, with the exception of the Sugarbush Inn. However, the areas are so close that either ski area can be reached from any lodge.

Mad River has a great selection of converted farmhouses that have   35 a cozy atmosphere and serve breakfast and dinner. The Mountain View Inn, with its rag rugs, homemade quilts, and antique beds, was our favorite for atmosphere. It also has a great reputation for food. Each room, though small, has a private bath, and costs $40, food included, per person. The Tucker Hill Lodge, with sixty kilometers of cross-country trails, is a little more polished but perhaps less personal. Doubles go for $48 per person, and larger rooms are available. The Millbrook, in need of some external refurbishing, costs $40 per person or $68 for a weekend plan. Serving a younger crowd, The Snuggery has its own restaurant/bar and hot tub located in a silo. The Schultzes run a popular bed-and-breakfast establishment a few miles down the road in Moretown. Now a major hotel, The Sugarbush Inn wants to be sophisticated, but merely seems snobby and impersonal. Rooms start at $72, with breakfast and dinner $27 extra. Lareau's, a genuine Victorian farmhouse between Sugarbush and Mad River, is a very pleasant bed-and-breakfast.

The Mad River Barn combines country dinners with up-to-date rooms. It's also the base for sixty kilometers of trails. The converted farmhouse has rooms as modern as any condominium's. Dinner is served in a traditional setting, and there's a popular afternoon bar upstairs.

The Battleground is a set of somewhat overpriced condominiums very close to Mad River. The Garrison is a very weird set of shabby apartments two stories high surrounding an indoor pool. Twelve people can stay in a four-bedroom place for five days for $13 per person, per night. For a smaller group, two people can have a studio with a kitchen for $25 a night. For large groups planning to stay a week, it's a great budget alternative.

For more hotel suggestions, see the Sugarbush listings.

ACCESSIBILITY

Mad River is four hours from Boston and six from New York. Amtrak and Greyhound service nearby Waterbury. People Express, US Air, and Air North now service Burlington, Vermont at their usual bargain fares. For example, People Express charges just $38 one-way from Newark, and $80 from Jacksonville, Florida during peak periods. And for $10, the Mad River Shuttle will take you to either ski area from the airport (phone 800–451–4580). The trip is just under an hour.

LISTINGS

Mad River
Waitsfield, VT   05673
802–496–3551

LIFT TICKET

$19 (holidays, $21)

RESTAURANTS

Beggar's Banquet, Fiddler's Green, 496–4485.
Blue Tooth, Sugarbush Access Road, 496–5100.
Chez Henri, Sugarbush Village, 583–2600.
China Barn, Route 17, 496–3579.
The Common Man, German Flats Road, 583–2800.
Gallagher's, Routes 17 and 100, 496–8800.
Michel's, Sugarbush Access Road, 583–3100.
Moose Lips, Routes 100 and 17, 496–8881.
Reveille, German Flats Road, 583–2255.
Sam Rupert's, Sugarbush Access Road, 583–2421.
Tucker Hill Lodge, Route 17, 496–3983.
The Waitsfield Inn, Route 100, 496–3979.

LODGING

Mountain View Inn, RFD Box 69, 496–2426.
Tucker Hill Lodge, Route 17, 496–3983 or toll-free 800–451–4580.
The Lareau Farm, Route 100, 496–4949.
Millbrook, RFD Box 62, 496–2405.
The Snuggery, RR 46a, 496–2322.
Sugarbush Inn, Route 100, Warren, 583–2301 or toll-free 800–451–4320.
Mad River Barn, Route 17, 496–3310.
The Garrison, Route 17, 495–2352.
Battleground, Route 17, 496–3034.
Schultzes', Route 100, Moretown, 496–2366.

MOUNT SNOW

As the southernmost Vermont ski area, Mount Snow has the advantage of being closer to New York and Boston, but its major drawback is its ski conditions, which can be way below Stowe's or even Stratton's.

Killington, which recently purchased the mountain, is trying to remedy the situation through snowmaking, but the best improvement they could make would be to increase the mountain's height, and knowing Killington, they might try. Mount Snow has challenging but short expert slopes, and a strong mix of beginner and intermediate trails.

Killington has also been trying to improve the resort's atmosphere by adding some class and local color. Several years ago, the crowd seemed to be filled with people who had accidentally wandered in from a low-budget cocktail party in Queens. Now Mount Snow seems to draw a crowd more interested in skiing than socializing. Most of the lodging is very reasonable, and prices often include breakfast and dinner.

THE SKIING

Mount Snow is composed of three connected mountain faces: Sunbrook area, Main Mountain, and the North Face. Each face generally caters to a different level skier. Sunbrook is home for beginners, with some long, wandering trails and more direct intermediate runs. An enclosed chair and a triple chair run to the top of Main Mountain, which adjoins the Sunbrook area. The tops of these intermediate trails are narrow and at times steep; at the bottom, they're easy cruising. To the right is North Face, which really is a separate area. Slalom Glade and P.D.F. are two stiff challenges, and Jaws of Death is no slouch. The other expert trails are challenging (akin to Stratton's) but far from overwhelming.

Mount Snow has eighteen chairlifts, including two bubble-enclosed lifts, and a total of fifty-two trails (liberally counted). Expect crowds on the slopes. All but a dozen or so trails have snowmaking (including most of the expert runs), so ice is usually kept to a minimum.

THE TOWN/NIGHTLIFE

Most of the action occurs at the restaurants along the nine-mile stretch of Route 100 between Mount Snow and Wilmington. Poncho's Wreck serves good Mexican food in a decor of sea-wreck memorabilia, with live entertainment nightly. Another favorite is Deacon's Den, a casual spot with a pool table and nightly entertainment. The wooden floors and walls covered with a collection of signs give the restaurant a distinctly local flavor. Nightly entertainment is available as well at the Andiron Lodge.

Although dining at your lodge may be available, you may want to explore Mount Snow's variety of good restaurants. Dimly lit by candles, Mainstreets in Wilmington is partially heated by an old potbelly stove. Dinners range from $6 to $16. The Deacon's Den is known for its live music and half-price pizza special on Thursdays, as well as a full range of sandwiches, subs, and homemade specials. The Cup and Saucer Coffee Shoppe caters mostly to locals and a few stray skiers lucky enough to stumble in. It serves classic diner food—eggs, omelettes, sandwiches, burgers, and such. The Roadhouse, a renovated farmhouse, is one of the more elegant restaurants in town. Complete dinners run $10 to $15. The owners of the Hermitage Inn raise all the pheasant, quail, duckling, and trout that they serve. You can dine on steak and seafood in an old sawmill at the Old Red Mill.

LODGING

Many of Mount Snow's lodgings include breakfast and dinner at quite reasonable prices. Just two miles from the ski area, the Snow Den Inn is a small country inn with nine rooms, great food, and a friendly atmosphere. All the beds are decorated with homemade quilts, and many rooms have fireplaces. A weekend here costs $75, while a five-day stay costs $128. The Misty Mountain Lodge, another country inn, has family-style, home-cooked meals. A weekend stay costs $42. The Old Red Mill, mentioned above for its restaurant, rests in the center of Wilmington on the Deerfield River. A weekend costs $40, not including meals.

The Viking Motel and Ski Lodge has rooms and efficiency apartments. Ski weekends with meals cost $40. A large lodge with a lounge and restaurant, The Andirons costs $100 for a weekend, including meals.

The Lodge at Mount Snow, a first-class facility at the base of the mountains, runs $98 for a ski weekend.

Condominiums are another option. The Timber Creek is a new set of condos with fireplaces, skating, and cross-country terrain. They are located just a few minutes from the slopes. Right next door are the Snow Tree Condominiums and Snow Mountain Village. They range from studios to townhouses and from $60 to $230.

ACCESSIBILITY

Mount Snow is about a four-and-a-half hour drive from New York. The nearest airports are in Albany (an hour and a half away) and Hartford (two hours away). Greyhound provides bus service to Wilmington.

LISTINGS

Mount Snow Ski Area
135L Mountain Road
Mount Snow, VT   05356
802–464–3333
Lodging: 802–464–8501

LIFT TICKET

$22 weekdays, $25 weekends and holidays

RESTAURANTS AND BARS

Deacon's Den, Route 100, 464–9361.
Poncho's Wreck, south of light on Route 100, 464–9320.
The Andirons, Route 100, 464–2114.
Mainstreets, West Main Street, 464–3183.
The Dover Forge Restaurant, Route 100, 464–2114.
The Cup and Saucer Coffee Shoppe, Route 100, 464–5813.
The Roadhouse, Route 100, 464–5017.
The Hermitage Inn, Coldbrook Road, 464–3759.
Old Red Mill, intersection of Routes 9 and 100, 464–3700.

LODGING

Snow Den Inn, P.O. Box 615, West Dover, 464-9355.

Misty Mountain Lodge, Stowe Hill Road, Wilmington, 464-3961.

Old Red Mill, Route 100, Wilmington, 464-3700.

The Viking Motel and Ski Lodge, Box 236, Wilmington, 464-5608.

Andirons, Route 100, West Dover, 464-2114.

The Lodge at Mount Snow, P.O. Box 755, North Dover, 464-5112 or toll-free 800-451-4289.

Timber Creek Condominiums, 100 Mountain Road, 464-3333 or toll-free 800-451-4211.

Snow Tree Condominiums and Snow Mountain Village, 100 Mountain Road, 464-3333 or toll-free 800-451-4211.

OKEMO

Everything's up to date in Okemo. Purchased in 1982 by new owners who intend to convert this sleepy little ski area into one of New England's largest resorts, it already has a new triple chairlift, eight new trails, new snowmaking equipment, and numerous condominiums. And before long there will be seventeen more trails, five more lifts, and over fifty condos. Not to mention the blitz of advertising to attract the busloads of skiers from New York. And the skiers are paying for it—lift tickets now cost $23.

Is this all for the better? Does the world need another Stratton? It depends on whom you ask. Many of the locals and families who own second homes in the area liked Okemo the way it was: uncrowded, inexpensive, and friendly. It offered a low-key alternative to nearby Killington and Stratton. But it's hard to argue against the expansion: the triple chair is long, fast, and convenient, and the mountain has room for new trails.

But ultimately the question is whether the mountain has enough trails for the newly installed lifts, and whether it has adequate snow. Okemo claims it has fifty-three trails, but this seems like an exaggeration. We've seen longer condo driveways.

In the midst of scenic Vermont, surrounded by lovely colonial villages, Okemo has a supply of condominiums and houses at the base of the mountain. You'll find the mountain mainly intermediate, with a mix of 30 percent beginner, 50 percent more difficult, and 20 percent most difficult. And the expert trails are far from intimidating—most would be labeled "intermediate" at other mountains.

THE SKIING

Okemo has many Poma lifts, the long rods with circular seats that you straddle, and you'll find them faster than the chairlifts and fun to ride. Three start at the base of the mountain. The beginner Poma can be ridden for free, while two other Pomas parallel a chairlift and give access to the same terrain. The triple chair is also available to beginners, who can cruise the 4.5-mile Mountain Road trail, which is actually a road in the summer.

Experts will prefer the narrow, twisty, moguled trails at the top of the mountain, like Upper Chief and Upper War Dance. But Okemo is primarily an intermediate's mountain.

THE TOWN/NIGHTLIFE

Okemo doesn't sizzle after dark, but you'll find some fun bars and a few spots to dance. Go to Dad's, next to Okemo on the access road, for beers after skiing. They have several levels, a pool table and video games, and you'll find whatever and whomever you're looking for when the lifts close. In or near town on Main Street are Nikki's and The Pub. Nikki's is a bit trendy, and The Pub is, well, a pub. For dancing, drive a mile down to Proctorsville to The Block or head toward Londonderry (twenty-five minutes away) to The Mill.

While dining in Ludlow isn't highly elegant, it's usually filling. DJ's is inexpensive and serves huge portions. Nikki's, which is very in now, has a varied menu at reasonable prices. You can get good Italian food at Valente's. For more elegant food, dine at either Governor's Inn or Chez Renée.

LODGING

To get trailside accommodations in condominiums and private homes, contact Okemo's reservation service. The Chapman House, a bed-and-breakfast establishment, is the nearest public lodging, just 500 yards from the slopes. Friendly and informal, rooms cost $16 apiece for the first two people, and $10 for each additional guest during peak seasons. The owner runs the restaurant next door. The Inn Towne Motel is a modern place in the town's center which runs $50 a night for two in peak seasons. Kitchenettes are $9 extra. Also modern, but bland, the Winchester Inn-Motel and Timber Inn Motel serve breakfast and dinner at a charge of $40 per person for a double. A huge old converted mill in the center of town, the Mill Motel looks wonderful on the outside, but little creativity was exercised in the interior. A double is $48 on weekends, $60 during holidays; a two-bedroom suite runs $140 on weekends and $185 during holidays. For a less expensive stay, try the Abby Lyn Motel at $17.50 a night, including breakfast, and the Mill Pond Lodge at $15 a night.

The Castle Inn, a Victorian granite castle that looms over Route 103, was built by a former governor of Vermont in 1904. It has long, stately hallways that lead to cavernous bedrooms, and an elegant dining room. Next door is Castle Tennis with two indoor tennis courts. The Black River Inn with its antiques and relaxed, informal atmosphere is a bargain bed-and-breakfast at $20 a night. There are four bedrooms in the house and a "family annex" in back.

You can stay in town at the formal and elegant Governor's Inn, which costs about $50 for breakfast alone and $80 if dinner is included. Less expensive are the Inn at Weathersfield and the well-known Inn at Weston. There are many other colonial and Victorian homes that have been converted into hotels in Ludlow and the surrounding region.

LISTINGS

Okemo Ski Area
RFD 1
Ludlow, VT   05149
802–228–4041
Lodging: 802–228–5571

LIFT TICKET

$20 weekdays, $23 weekends and holidays

NIGHTLIFE

The Pub, 128 Main Street, 228–8646.
Nikki's, Routes 100 and 103, 228–7797.
Dad's, Access Road, 228–9820.
The Mill, 145 Main Street, 228–5566.

RESTAURANTS

DJ's, 146 Main Street, 228–5374.
Mama Valente's, 190 Main Street, 228–2671.
Chez Renée, 30 Pond St., 228–5354.
Governor's Inn, 86 Main Street, 228–8830.

LODGING

Abby Lyn Motel, Routes 106 and 10, North Springfield, 886–2223.
The Black River Inn, 100 Main St., Ludlow, 228–5585.
Castle Inn, Routes 103 and 131, Proctorsville, 226–7222.
The Chapman House, 44 Pond Street, Ludlow, 228–8632.
The Governor's Inn, 86 Main Street, Ludlow, 228–8830.
The Inn at Weathersfield, Route 106, Weathersfield, 263–9217.
The Inn Towne Motel, 12 Main Street, Ludlow, 228–8884.
The Mill Hotel, 145 Main Street, Ludlow, 228–5566.
Mill Pond Lodge, 82 Andover Street, Ludlow, 228–8926.
The Timber Inn Motel, Route 103 South, Ludlow, 228–8666.
The Winchester, 53 Main Street, Ludlow, 228–3841.

STOWE

Stowe earns its position in our ranking as number one in New England thanks to its combination of three mountains, an unspoiled setting, and a quaint New England town.

The main mountain, Mansfield, has a variety of expert and intermediate slopes. You won't find more challenging trails than Goat or Star this side of the Mississippi. The gondola serves an impressive array of intermediate terrain, with trails averaging over a mile in length. Spruce gives intermediates more room to wander, and thanks to recent expansion beginners can ski there, too.

But the real difference between Stowe and its nearest competitors, Killington and Sugarbush, is that Stowe still *feels* like a ski area—not a shopping center. No clusters of condos crowd the slopes; there is no ski village at the base of the mountain, and you don't see the busloads coming from New Jersey.

Lest we stand accused of working for Stowe's PR department, we should like to list Stowe's drawbacks. Stowe isn't cheap. The lift lines get very long. You have to take a shuttle between Spruce and Mansfield. It gets very cold. But especially on a weekday, either the gondola or the chair at Mansfield is the place to be.

THE SKIING

Feeling cocky since you cruised the expert trails at Stratton? Ever done one of the toughies at Sugarbush? Ready for the big time? Here it is—the Mount Mansfield chairlift. Star is a no-holds-barred, no-escape, expert plunge. Once you get on this run you can't escape onto any trails. It's narrow, steep, and treacherous. Goat is narrow and steep, too, and it slopes off 20 degrees to the left. These two trails are the last to open at Stowe. National, perhaps the most famous of the "super-expert" trails at Stowe, has a broad but steep top and huge moguls. Liftline, though not as glamorous as the rest, is a consistent challenge. Nosedive lost some of its challenge when it lost a few of its seven famous turns, but it's still tough at the top.

Off the same lift are several long, challenging intermediate runs: Center Line, Skimeister, and Charlie Lord. Finally there's the long beginner cruise, Toll Road, which leads down to Toll House.

The gondola is home for intermediates. Wander down from near the top of Vermont's tallest peak on long, intermediate trails like Gondola and Perry Merril. Chin Clip, the sole expert run, has some steep drops.

Spruce Peak is a great place for intermediates to practice—and avoid the lift lines. Sterling is a long, wandering trail, great to picnic on. Whirlaway and Smuggler's are two more advanced trails. Toll House used to be the beginner's terrain, but Stowe expanded Spruce, so that is now also the beginner's area.

During 1984, Stowe put in a chairlift from Toll House to Mansfield, and the resort plans to convert Toll House into a major condominium complex. The lift will let homeowners ride up to Mansfield and return via the Toll Road.

You can't talk about Stowe and avoid mentioning the lift lines. Spruce and Toll House rarely have any. Mount Mansfield's gondola sees forty-minute lines on weekends, and the chairlifts are getting close to that. The lines on the new chair are slightly shorter, but you won't get a blanket to keep warm as you do on the old line.

For those who like to go horizontally as well as vertically, Stowe, with over one hundred miles of connected trails, has the best cross-country skiing in Vermont. There is Edson Hill Manor, Stowe, and the Trapp Family Lodge (owned by the Trapps of *The Sound of Music* fame), all now linked by trails.

THE TOWN/NIGHTLIFE

After a long day of strenuous skiing, grab a drink at the lodge.

Then make a stop at the Matahorn, the ramshackle, raucous building on the right on your way down the mountain road. They sometimes put someone out in a clown costume or a bear suit to flag down drivers. You can dance to a live band in the late afternoon or early evening while you're having a drink.

For more dancing, head to either the Rusty Nail, Sister Kate's, or the Baggy Knees. Be sure and check to see who's playing—they sometimes have semi-big-time New England bands like NRBQ or Livingston Taylor. In general, the Rusty Nail gets more of the college crowd. If you're in the mood for a western-style bar, check out C. K. Clark's, an up-and-coming spot that sometimes has bands.

If skiing has worn you out, visit the refined Buttery at Topnotch, the very British Pub, or a restaurant/bar like the Three Green Doors.

RESTAURANTS

The list is good. Expensive but excellent, Ile de France has Stowe's best French cuisine. The Ten Acres, though a bit stuffy, has fine New England-style food.

Ten minutes down the road, the Golden Horn East serves superb veal and the Partridge Inn has great seafood. Both these restaurants are in the $10 to $15 range.

For an informal, less expensive meal try The Shed and Three Green Doors. Their atmosphere is wonderful, and they're fun for anyone.

Steen's, a step up, is run by the former chef of The Shed. Villa Tragadara is a quality Italian restaurant.

On the budget side, the Stoweaway or L'il Abner serve good Mexican food, while the Flying Tomato is the spot for pizza.

LODGING

Stowe's lodging has the drawback of being on the busy Mountain Road. However, there is much to choose from, so it's easy to find the right price and location.

Starting with the mountain, there's the very posh Inn at the Mountain, which will soon have its own chairlift to Mansfield. With meals, a room costs $78 per person in a double. Condos on the same location cost $130 a night.

The Ski Inn is an informal, family place. An attractive country inn just minutes from Mansfield, it's a bargain at $21 to $30, meals included. The Fiddler's Green Inn and the Siebeness Lodge nearby offer similar accommodations and prices. They feel more like homes than inns, and it's easy to hook into the cross-country trails from them. A step up is the Scandinavia Inn, which in addition to its lodge now has motel rooms and chalets.

The Edson Hill Manor—site of the winter scenes for the movie *The Four Seasons*—is a lovely country inn off Mountain Road. Rooms with meals run $45 to $65. In a similar price range, but a bit farther away and a little too pretentious for our tastes, is the Ten Acre Lodge. The Green Mountain Inn is formal and exquisite. Rooms run about $40 a night, meals not included. (All rates quoted above are per person, double occupancy.)

The nicest set of condominiums is Notchbrook Resort, just off Mountain Road. The condos, which run from $90 to over $200 a day, have a more secluded feel than most.

Mountain Road has many motels. Though fairly similar, some of the better ones are the Alpine Motor Lodge, the Town and Country Motor Lodge, the Stoweflake Resort, and the Golden Eagle Motor Inn. The first three, with meals, are in the $40 to $50 price range, and the Golden Eagle costs $25 to $35. The Buccaneer, Die Alpenrose, Innsbruck, and Hob Knob are even less expensive. Check with the Stowe Area Association. Again, rates are per person for sharing a double.

Finally, there are dormitories. Round Hearth Lodge is probably the best known, with hot tubs, game rooms, and the like. The Winterhaus is just a bit up the road. Both cost about $20 a night with meals, and are more interesting places to stay than the State of Vermont Ski Dorm.

ACCESSIBILITY

Stowe fanatics could once be recognized from their tired eyes, the result of the six-hour trek from New York. But with the growth of the

Burlington Airport and bargain airlines like People Express and US Air, Stowe has become a cheap flight away. A shuttle bus makes the forty-five-minute trip from the airport. Amtrak and Vermont Transit buses also stop at Burlington.

LISTINGS

Stowe Ski Resort
106 Mountain Road
Stowe, VT   05672
802-253-7311

For Lodging

Stowe Area Association
Box 1230
Stowe, VT   05672
802-253-7321

LIFT TICKET

$24

RESTAURANTS/NIGHTLIFE

The Matterhorn, Mountain Road, 253-9198.
Sister Kate's, Mountain Road, 253-8897.
The Rusty Nail, Mountain Road, 253-8107.
Baggy Knees, Mountain Road, 253-8728.
C. K. Clark's, Stowe Center Complex, Mountain Road, 253-9300.
Three Green Doors, Mountain Road, 253-8979.
The Pub at Stowe, Mountain Road, 253-8977.
Ile de France, Mountain Road, 253-7751.
Ten Acres, Barrows Road, 253-7638.
Partridge Inn, Mountain Road, 253-8000.
The Shed, Mountain Road, 253-4364.
Steen's, Mountain Road, 253-7269.
Villa Tragadara, Route 100, Waterbury, 244-5288.
Stoweaway, Mountain Road, 253-7574.
Li'l Abner's, Cottage Club Road, 253-9281.
Flying Tomato, Mountain Road, 253-4646.
Swisspot, Main Street, 253-4622.

LODGING

Edson Hill Manor, Edson Hill Road, 253-7371.
Fiddler's Green Inn, Mountain Road, 253-8124.
Green Mountain Inn, Main Street, 253-7301.
Ski Inn, Mountain Road, 253-4050.

Ten Acres Lodge, Luce Hill and Barrows Road, 253-7638.
Alpine Motor Lodge, Mountain Road, 253-7700.
Buccaneer Motel and Ski Lodge, Mountain Road, 253-4772.
Die Alpenrose, Mountain Road, 253-7277.
Golden Eagle, Mountain Road, 800-626-1010 or 253-4811.
Hob Knob Inn, Mountain Road, 253-8549.
Stoweflake Resort, Mountain Road, 253-7355.
Innsbruck Inn, Mountain Road, 253-8582.
Town & Country Motor Lodge, Mountain Road, 253-7595.
Round Hearth Lodge, Mountain Road, 253-7223.
Winterhaus, Mountain Road, 253-7731.
The Inn at the Mountain, Mountain Road, 253-7311.
Notch Brook Resort, Notch Brook Road, 253-4882.

STRATTON

For southern Vermont, Stratton is big time. Million-dollar homes line its gentle slopes, and Porsches and Peugeot station wagons fill the parking lot. Stratton is the status symbol for the suburban family on the move.

Besides the fact that it's a big intermediate mountain for the upscale family, Stratton leaves us unmoved. If you're a beginner or intermediate, great. Otherwise, the trails won't challenge anyone beyond a solid intermediate; Killington, Stowe, and Sugarbush are better mountains at almost any level. Stratton's lift lines are long, and though the valley boasts good restaurants, the nightlife is far from sizzling.

Stratton draws its crowds because it's close and so "pleasant." Only four hours from New York, it has retained its unspoiled air. During the day, you can cruise the expert slopes, feeling like a pro. At night, you can feel safe, knowing that the two hottest nightspots double as country inns.

THE SKIING

It's great to be a beginner or especially an intermediate at Stratton. There are three chairs almost exclusively for beginners, and if you're a novice, you can certainly handle a lot of the intermediate terrain, such as Suntanner. You should beware, though, of taking Work Road to Wanderer—it can be frightening when it's icy.

Most of the expert terrain is on the upper half of the mountain, which is served by three chairs. But since a good intermediate can ski many of the expert trails—like Tamarack and Polar Bear—you'll still find long lift lines. Spruce is probably the most challenging expert trail. The Sun Bowl has shorter lift lines on its mix of novice and intermediate runs.

THE TOWN/NIGHTLIFE

Stratton has no real town. Clustered at the base of the ski area are condos and a few hotels with restaurants and bars. Bondville, at the bottom of the access road, consists of a gas station, a grocery store, and a post office. Manchester Center, the nearest town, is a good twenty minutes away. To get to the scattered nightlife you'll need a car.

There are two places to go dancing—Haig's or the Red Fox Inn.
50   Haig's is a fancy disco complete with flashing floor and draws a

preppy New York crowd, while the Red Fox, which has a bar and restaurant set in a barn, draws locals, ski instructors, and out-of-staters. There are two bars on either side of the access road, the River Café and Tumbledown's. The lodges at the mountain's base have quieter bars, sometimes with entertainment on weekends. A few other nightspots are listed under Bromley, but they're a good thirty minutes away.

The Red Fox is a fine place to take the family for food. Located in a barn complete with farm implements, a good meal will cost $10 to $12. You can get a good steak and all you can eat of soup and salad at Haig's. For quiche and big sandwiches try the River Café. Tumbledown's serves everything from steak and seafood to burgers and ribs. You can get good continental as well as Austrian fare at the Birkenhaus and the Liftline Lodge at the base of Stratton. For further selections see the Bromley chapter. The Newfane Inn, a lovely colonial inn on the green next to some equally lovely churches, is a bit of a trip, but well worth it.

LODGING

There are a number of hotels, condominiums, and houses at the base of Stratton, and nearly all are within walking distance of the slopes. The newly renovated Stratton Mountain Inn has elegant dining, plus all the frills of a first-class resort. Rooms start at $47.50. The Birkenhaus and Liftline Lodge keep the old Tyrolean spirit alive. They supply two meals and run $120 to $140 per person for a weekend.

A bit further down the road is the Chalet Wendland, which sleeps six and serves meals. A weekend runs $66 per person.

Haig's, a country inn, is on the access road. Rooms run from $30 to $48. For a nice retreat, try the Red Fox Inn, located on a back road. The Bear Creek is a new hotel/condo combination nearby. A weekend, with meals, costs $110.

Other spots are at least fifteen minutes away. For more suggestions, see the Bromley chapter. A bargain on Route 30 is the Vagabond Ski Lodge, where bunks cost $12 a night, weekend or weekday. Stratton Mountain Reservations can handle bookings at all these establishments.

ACCESSIBILITY

Stratton is about four hours from New York City and three hours from Boston. Amtrak can take you to Bellows Falls, which is a bus ride away. Vermont Transit buses also pull in frequently to Manchester Center, which is twenty-five minutes away. The nearest airport is in Keene, NH, fifty miles away.

LISTINGS

Stratton Mountain
Stratton Mountain, VT   05155
802-297-2200
Lodging: 802-824-6915

LIFT TICKET

$25 (valid also at Bromley)

RESTAURANTS/NIGHTLIFE

Haig's, Route 30, 297-1300.
The Red Fox Inn, Winhall Hollow Road, 297-2543.
Tumbledown's, Route 30, 297-1234.
River Café, Route 30, 297-1010.
Liftline Lodge, Stratton Mountain, 297-2600.
Birkenhaus, Stratton Mountain, 297-2000.

LODGING

Chalet Wendland, RFD, Jamaica, 874-4088.
Red Fox Inn, Winhall Hollow Road, 297-2543.
The Birkenhaus, Stratton Mountain, 297-2000.
Bear Creek, Route 30, Rawsonville, 297-1700.
Haig's, Route 30, 297-1300.
Liftline Lodge, Stratton Mountain, 297-2600.
Stratton Mountain Inn, Stratton Mountain, 297-2500.
Vagabond Ski Lodge, Route 30, East Jamaica, 874-4096.

SUGARBUSH

Nothing negative we say is going to alter Sugarbush's tremendous appeal, so we'll start with the positive—Sugarbush has great trails, great restaurants, and a great night-life. But unfortunately, it's become overrun with condominiums and buses. At the base of the mountain rests Sugarbush Village, a massive complex that sleeps 3,000. You may not believe you're in the wilds of Vermont. Parts of Sugarbush and the surrounding lodges resemble Fort Lauderdale more than Vermont, and that, of course, is one of the main reasons for the resort's appeal to some.

Like some of Fort Lauderdale's bars, with their wet T-shirt contests and other circus acts, Sugarbush will do anything for a crowd. One good draw is the "vertical feet" contest—classes are challenged to see how many feet they can cover in two hours. So if you get run down by an intermediate skier hurtling downhill out of control, you have "Sugarbush Action Week" to thank.

Sugarbush is divided into two areas, Sugarbush proper and Sugarbush North (formerly Glen Ellen). Although the shuttle ride is short between them, most skiers stay on the main mountain. Sugarbush has thirty-six trails, while Sugarbush North counts forty, because Sugarbush is more honest about counting its trails than anyplace around. If it wanted, the mountain management could add a dozen trails or so by counting small connectors and such.

Sugarbush and Mad River share much of their nightlife, lodging, and restaurants. There are several pleasant country inns near Mad River, while Sugarbush has an abundance of condos and budget motels. Sugarbush also has a fully developed sports center with tennis, swimming, squash, and racquetball (and in the summer there is golf and polo). Mad River and Sugarbush combine for a great resort, perhaps New England's finest; it's a shame Sugarbush has become so commercial.

For accessibility, restaurants, and nightlife, see the Mad River chapter. Country inns and lodges that are closer to Mad River are listed under Mad River; lodging closer to Sugarbush is listed in this section.

THE SKIING

Sugarbush has great expert, solid intermediate, and adequate beginner terrain. Sugarbush North is stronger in the beginner category. It   53 has good intermediate skiing as well, and a somewhat disorganized expert area.

Sugarbush is one of New England's best-designed mountains. The resort's centerpiece is a 9,600-foot gondola that services some intermediate but mainly expert terrain. The expert trails are fairly narrow but not too steep. Jester is an enjoyable trail that leads to intermediate skiing.

To the right of the gondola is Sugarbush's nicely segregated beginner/intermediate area. A chair services the beginner area, while a chair/Poma combination takes you to a nice array of intermediate trails.

To the left are the Spring Fling triple chair and the Valley House chair, which, though short, have some of the best and bumpiest runs around. Steep and bumpy, Stein's is one of New England's most challenging trails. The Spring chair serves some intermediate and beginner terrain.

Halfway up and to the right of the gondola, Castlerock is expert only. Though you'll find steeper trails, these are narrow and bumpy. For instance, Lift Line is very steep in sections, and Rumble is steep and narrow. It takes nerve as much as skill to ski them.

Once a low-key, often overlooked ski area, Sugarbush North (Glen Ellen to those with memory) still has the shorter lift lines. With a vertical drop second only to Killington's, the mountain unfortunately suffers from a roller-coaster effect—flat at times, steep at others. The long runs off the Mountain Chair end up as nearly flat beginner trails. Sugarbush North does have Black Diamond and Upper FIS, two trails that are steep as they come, but they're short. The mountain has a large collection of intermediate trails, but it may take a while to find the ones you like. Trails like Chicane to Lower FIS are great wander-

SUGARBUSH, VERMONT

ing routes from the top, while Inverness is a more traditional, wide trail.

LODGING

To say Sugarbush has condos is an understatement. Sugarbush Village, within skiing distance (remember the 3,000 beds?), costs between $86 and $110 for one bedroom, and two bedrooms run between $132 and $172. At the same price, Snow Creek Condominiums, at the triple chair, is a lovely set of two-bedroom units. Another popular condo is South Village. Off the mountain, but with breakfast and dinner, Powderhound has one-bedroom units.

All accommodations for these units are handled by Sugarbush Reservations, which also has a package including lodging at the village for two from Sunday through Friday with five-and-a-half days' skiing for $399.

Sugarbush also has a number of standard hotels, but for a little more money you might as well stay at a country inn (see Mad River chapter).

The least expensive package is a ski weekend at the Lantern Lodge. In the spring, it will book four college students per room, serve continental breakfast and Saturday dinner, and include lift tickets for just $79 per person. Sergeant Pepper's is a nicer place. You'll get a bunk and breakfast for $40 a weekend. Another cheap student place with bunks is The Lodge. The White Horse Inn is modern and pleasant, with a room costing $40, and breakfast and dinner an extra $10. Two people can stay at the Golden Horse for $72, including breakfast. The Golden Lion, a friendly establishment, runs just $42 for a double per night. Sixty dollars per person will get you a room for a weekend at the Alpen, and for $36 more you'll receive breakfast and dinner.

LISTINGS

Sugarbush Valley Ski Resort
Sugarbush Valley, VT   05674
802–583–2381
Lodging: 800–451–5030

LIFT TICKET

$25

LODGING

Sergeant Pepper's, German Flats Road, Warren, 583–2255.
The Alpen, Route 100, Waitsfield, 496–3416.
Golden Lion Inn, P.O. Box 336, Warren, 496–3084.   55

The Golden Horse Lodge, Sugarbush Access Road, Warren, 583-3200.

The Lodge, Sugarbush Road, Warren, 583-2474.

The White Horse Inn, German Flats Road, Waitsfield, 496-2476.

Lantern Lodge (contact Paul Tetreault, 190 Chestnut Street, Holyoke, Massachusetts, 413-532-9469 or toll-free 800-628-9530).

WHITEFACE

The spirit of the 1980 Winter Olympics is still alive at Whiteface Mountain—you'll see signs asking you to watch out for athletes in training. The world's largest ice complex and the Olympic Authority building dominate the center of the town. Besides skiing at Whiteface, you can skate on the speed-skating oval, take a bobsled run, or try the Olympic cross-country ski trail.

But Lake Placid remains very much the same despite its fleeting fame. The town has made practical use of its former Olympic facilities, for instance converting a dorm into a prison. The town still consists of Main Street. Whiteface is separated from the big, fashionable resorts in Vermont by more than Lake Champlain.

THE SKIING

Surprisingly for an Olympic-class resort, Whiteface has only nine lifts and twenty-eight trails. From its 4,807-foot peak there is a spectacular view across Lake Champlain. The variety of trails will challenge even the experienced skier. However, owing to the height there are high winds, and Whiteface has problems keeping snow. So the expert trails, hard enough without the frequent ice, earn their reputation as among the toughest in the East.

Organized into separate sections for beginners, intermediates, and experts, trails are well marked. Don't ignore the Experts Only signs before you head up to the upper slopes.

From the bottom, the slalom courses for Olympic, World Cup, and other competitions on Mountain Run and Parkway look fairly easy. But try them race-style—without stopping—and you'll gain some respect. If these trails don't challenge you, the steepness of the expert trails off the peak will.

Coming down the lower runs off the two main chairs is easier—excellent snowmaking and grooming make them a pleasure for any skier. Beginners should still be somewhat cautious and may prefer to ski at Olympic Acres, an area off to the side which has only novice runs.

Lift lines are rare at Whiteface, with pile-ups occurring only on the #2 chair on weekends. Lift tickets are a bargain: college students under twenty-one can purchase the $15 junior weekend rate.

THE TOWN/NIGHTLIFE

To discuss the town, we must begin with the Olympic facilities. Mount Van Hoevenberg Recreation Area specializes in nordic skiing and offers a guide to the beautiful countryside surrounding Lake Placid. For experts there are the ten-kilometer Porter Mountain loops; the estimated times of these racing trails are posted, so you can test yourself. Rent some skis at Cunningham's Ski Barn, get a map, and explore.

Only an Olympic town could offer you various types of sledding as an organized activity. Try the special tobogganing run which goes right down to the frozen lake for a slick finish. You can take a dogsled ride around Mirror Lake or rent a team for the day or an overnight expedition. If you think roller-coaster rides are kid's stuff, try the bobsled run. The passenger sled flies down the refrigerated course with its fourteen-foot vertical drops and 180-degree curves. Remember: in competitions, hitting the break pedal is grounds for disqualification.

Parasailing or ski-mobiling around Mirror Lake offers still more adrenalin surges. At a slower pace, try ice-skating around the speed oval. Or if you're sad you missed the Olympics, Lake Placid still has plenty of Olympic-quality athletes around. Pick up a local newspaper or weekly calendar to find out what skiing, speed-skating, luge, ski jumping, and hockey events (among others) are scheduled.

Nights don't last long in a town where everyone burns more calories during the day than they can drink in an evening. The Shed has some amazing drinks which you will dream about on cold chairlift rides, and if the sun is still out, visit the Artist's Café and get a view of people parasailing or dogsledding on the lake.

Later, the Cottage is the spot for relaxed conversation and jukebox dancing. To meet the athletes, play some pool or toss some darts at the Arena. The Lowlife is just that. For dancing and live music, go to Mud Puddles, the town's main nightspot, or the Lake Placid Club, although these spots are a little weak on ambiance. The clientele, as well as the atmosphere, seems a bit imported.

RESTAURANTS

Lake Placid has a good variety of restaurants with reasonable prices. The Steak 'n' Stinger's home cooking and the Cascade's steak—the biggest in town—are the local favorites (and we agree). Frederick's and Le Chalet also feature continental cooking, but at much higher prices. The Alpine Cellar in the Edelweiss Motel serves German specialties that satisfy even the native Germans who eat there. The chili at the Cottage has a lot of bite, and the Woodshed, Casey's, and the Artist's Cafe all have decent spaghetti, ribs, and such, but are better known for their drinks and decor.

LODGING

While Lake Placid doesn't specialize in old-style country inns, it does have a number of interesting and relatively inexpensive places to stay. The Lake Placid Club is a rambling old lakeside structure with every sort of shop, facility, and type of room available, from $19 dorm rooms to condominiums. It is definitely the place to stay for the college and younger set, and package deals are easily arranged. The nightlife is livelier here, and on off-season nights you can brighten up your nights in the game room or theater.

If you want to experiment (or be experimented on), check in as a guinea pig at the Hotel Saranac of Paul Smith's College. This old, 250–room hotel located in Saranac serves as a training ground for the restaurant and hotel management students at the college. Rooms and meals are cheap at $20 a night.

The Mirror Lake Inn in town has a spectacular view. It has a gym, sauna, whirlpool, and happy hour. Rooms cost $40 to $60. There are a Hilton and Holiday Inn in town with nice views of the lake. They are in the $40 to $60 range.

The bed-and-breakfast generally offers cosier, quieter, and usually less expensive accommodations. North Country Bed and Breakfast, a reservation service, will find you something to match your rooming needs. Rooms run from $10 to $100 a night. Young's Tourist Home in the center of town is a lovely and inexpensive place to stay. Further away in Keene there is the Bark Eater, a 150-year-old farmhouse with eight rooms for guests. Both charge just $26 a night.

Inexpensive beds and the occasional kitchenette can be found in any of the numerous motels lining the roads leading into Lake Placid. The least expensive, however, is the Sports Palace. At $12 a night for a bunk (you provide sleeping bag) you get a full breakfast with lots of eggs and pancakes. This is one of the best deals around—if you don't mind the bunk.

ACCESSIBILITY

Lake Placid is about a six-hour drive from New York City. Buses run from New York to Lake Placid, as does Amtrak. Clinton-Aero, a commuter airline, flies from New York and other cities to Lake Clear airport (twenty minutes away).

LISTINGS

Whiteface Mountain
Wilmington, NY   12997
518–946–2223

Olympic Ski Authority
Olympic Center
Lake Placid, NY 12946
518-523-1655

Lake Placid Chamber of Commerce
Olympic Arena
Lake Placid, NY 12946
518-523-2445

LIFT TICKET

$15 weekdays, $19 weekends and holidays

BARS AND NIGHTLIFE

The Arena, 220 Main Street, 523-2955.
Casey's, 444 Main Street, 523-2357.
The Cottage, 35 Mirror Lake Drive, 523-9845.
The Lowlife, 336 Main Street, 523-8074.
Lake Placid Club, Mirror Lake Drive, 523-3361.
Mud Puddles, 3 School Drive, 523-4446.
The Woodshed, 237 Main Street, 523-9470.

RESTAURANTS

The Alpine Cellar, 86 Wilmington Road, 523-2180.
The Artist's Café, 1 Main Street, 523-9493.
Casey's Olde Towne Pub, 444 Main Street, 523-2357.
The Cottage, 35 Mirror Lake Drive, 523-9845.
The Chalet, Mirror Lake Drive, 523-2241.
Cascade, Cascade Road, Route 73, 523-2130.
Frederick's, Signal Hill Road, 523-2310.
Steak 'n' Stinger, 15 Cascade Road, 523-9927.
The Woodshed, 237 Main Street, 523-9470.

LODGING

The Bark Eater, Allstead Road, Keene, 576-2221.
Lake Placid Hilton, Saranac Avenue, 523-4411.
Holiday Inn, Olympic Drive, Lake Placid, 523-2556.
Hotel Saranac (of Paul Smith's College), Main Street, Saranac,
    891-2200.
Lake Placid Club, Mirror Lake Drive, 523-3361.
Mirror Lake Inn, Mirror Lake Drive, 523-2544.
Sports Palace, 3 Highland Place, 523-2377.

Young's Tourist Home, Parkside Avenue, 523-3247.

For further bed and breakfast suggestions, contact

North Country Bed and Breakfast Reservation Service
The Barn
Box 286
Lake Placid, NY   12496
518–523–3793

Steamboat Springs ●

● Winter Park

* Vail ● Copper Mtn.
●

Keystone ●

★ DENVER

Aspen ●

● Breckenridge

■ Crested Butte

■ Colorado Springs

■ Grand Junction

● Telluride

COLORADO

Purgatory ●

■ Durango

Colorado

For most Americans, skiing means Colorado. Vail and Aspen, the giants of the ski world, have, for better or worse, done more to shape the image of the sport than any other ski area. Thanks to the "Vailspen" mystique, many novices view skiing as a sport for the upper classes, the rich and the famous, the stars and the athletic yuppies—anyone who can drop a few thousand on plane fare, a condo, a bunch of elegant meals, sleek new equipment, and chic new ski wear.

At best, this image has given the sport an aura of sophistication and credibility that makes it very alluring. At worst, it has prevented millions of folks from skiing because they think they wouldn't quite fit in with the glamorous types on the slopes.

But a close look at all the major Colorado ski areas destroys this elitist myth—a ski vacation in Colorado can be within most everyone's budget, and you don't need the latest neon ski pants to buy a lift ticket. Levis over a pair of long underwear will suffice (and at some areas, is preferred).

Aspen is probably the king of the hill in Colorado. With its four fine mountains in close proximity and a dazzling collection of restaurants and bars and beautiful young singles, Aspen is tough to top if you're under thirty-five. So Vail doesn't try. Rather, it's content to lure the over-thirty-five crowd, the folks who have, to some degree or another, "made it" (or want to mingle with those who have). With Jerry Ford as its principal spokesman, Vail offers a large, conservative, boring ski village and an enormous mountain with enough trails to satisfy any skier for a full week.

As Ford is to Vail, so Billy Kidd, the former ski champion and cowboy/showman extraordinaire, is to Steamboat Springs. Even though this resort has undergone great expansion, it hasn't lost its genuinely friendly western atmosphere. A favorite among Denver residents, Winter Park charges low prices and has a surprising variety of trails. Breckenridge, long in its neighbors' shadows, has become much more challenging due to its recent major addition of trails. Keystone, 63 a convenient family resort owned by Ralston-Purina, has well-packaged vacations. Telluride is great for experts, and you'll love the old mining town. Crested Butte offers the best of both worlds—a fine intermediate mountain with a condo city adjacent to the ski area, and a lovely old mining town about two miles down the road. Purgatory, which is beginning a $250-million expansion, could blossom into a major force by the end of the decade. At the moment, it's a good—but not great—mountain with a fun town twenty-five miles away. Copper Mountain, within shouting distance of Vail, is an aesthetically pleasing mountain and town, with equally pleasing skiing.

ASPEN

Aspen is to skiing as Fort Lauderdale is to Spring Break. Both towns shine like disco strobes in the night, beckoning the young, the decadent, the stars, and the groupies to the daily ritual of spending money, skiing, frolicking, spending money, eating dinner, spending money, and drinking and dancing. And the next day, doing it all again.

Especially the spending-money part. In Aspen, you'll probably see more furs and jewelry than you've ever seen before. And then when you get off the slopes . . .

Some reports maintain Aspen has the highest cost of living in the continental United States. But who in his right mind would want to live there? The phrase "Never trust anyone over thirty" never caught on in Aspen because there's no one there over thirty. Once you begin your fourth decade, civility demands that you ship out quietly and either get a real job or move to Vail.

But students flock to Fort Lauderdale for the beach and the sun first, and for the nightlife second. The same goes for Aspen—people come to Aspen to ski. Four separate mountains, each with its own personality, will keep skiers of all levels content.

But navigating the mountains can be a bit tricky. The Aspen Skiing Company operates three of the four—Aspen Mountain (also known as Ajax), Buttermilk, and Snowmass—and you can ski all three with one lift ticket. To tackle the fourth, Aspen Highlands, owned by the Aspen Highlands Skiing Corporation, you'll need a separate ticket, and the Aspen Skiing Company will sell you an Aspen Highlands ticket only on special request when you purchase your ticket.

The two companies have a rocky history, wavering from cooperation to out-and-out feuding. A few years ago, they offered a four-mountain pass, and Aspen Highlands received its share of the take. Skiers loved it, but the Aspen Skiing Company charged Highlands with inflating its skier numbers in order to get a bigger cut of the sales. The Skiing Company dropped the four-mountain pass, and in 1981, Highlands sued for unfair competition and won a $7.5-million judgment. The Skiing Company appealed, of course, and the case is still in the courts. So the two companies are not on good terms these days.

THE SKIING

Buttermilk. The "kids' mountain"—offers a number of wide, gentle runs for beginners and intermediates. It's a family and training moun-

tain, where experts can perfect their racing techniques on uncrowded and well-maintained slopes that are designed simply and efficiently. Buttermilk is also a good mountain to ski first if you're not accustomed to the high altitudes. It has an excellent ski school as well. Solid intermediates should have little trouble with the black runs, and, in fact, Buttermilk is a good choice for intermediates when the other mountains are teeming with skiers. But if you don't like seeing runny noses or hunting for yet another lost mitten, stay away.

Aspen Highlands. It's a little difficult to get there, but it's worth it. Why? Is it Floradora? Is it a titillating stretch of slope? No, it's Gretl Uhl's apple strudel at the Merry-Go-Round Restaurant. There's no better way to end a day on the slopes than to buy a lift ticket, ride up to the restaurant, have a piece of strudel, and simply ride back down.

Entertainment is as important at Aspen Highland as skiing. Every day at one o'clock, members of the ski patrol stage a stupendous jump over the terrace of the Cloud Nine Restaurant. And on Fridays, there's a freestyle skiing competition on Floradora. With student discounts, half-day tickets for morning and afternoon, and a family plan, prices can be very reasonable.

Aspen Highlands is a well-balanced mountain offering awesome views from its peak and runs for skiers of all levels. There are challenging intermediate runs like Floradora, as well as good expert runs (although these are a bit short). One of the most stunning lift rides we encountered in our travels is on the Loges Peak lift, #4, taking you over an avalanche chute and some spectacular cliffs.

So don't overlook Aspen Highlands. The skiing is fine, the strudel unbelievable, and if you're tired of Snowmass but not yet ready for Ajax, it's the place to go.

Snowmass. The only drawback to Snowmass is its distance from Aspen—twenty minutes by car—and once you get there you have to park well below the slopes and then take a shuttle. But so what. It's a great mountain for the average skier, and is perfect if you have a week or two to spend on the slopes. Like Vail, Snowmass proved that the real profit in the ski business comes not from the experts, but rather the average skier who can take off a week or two every year. The average skier is looking for diverse and challenging terrain without risking life and limb in front of the kids. If that sounds like you, then Snowmass is probably the finest ski mountain in the world.

Unfortunately, we're not telling the world anything new—Snowmass can get very crowded, and we don't have any neat tips on avoiding lines. All we can suggest is that you get there early on weekends and holidays.

Snowmass is the intermediates' mountain *par excellence.* Two-thirds of the trails are blue; 22 percent are black. And even the less experienced skier has plenty of room to traverse the wide-open slopes. The mountain resembles a miniature Vail, with dozens of trails and thirteen lifts. Study your map and chart your runs to avoid repetition and frustration. For the best view of the mountain, ski the runs off the top of Elk Camp. The six trails are enjoyable and not too varied. Naked Lady and Slider, off lift 15, will be a thrill for the lower intermediate, and you can prove you're in shape on the 3.7-mile Green Cabin run—solid intermediate all the way from top to bottom. The most popular runs on the mountain are from Big Burn, but keep your speed up as you go over the trestle at the bottom or you'll be poling.

Talk about jammed—try Max Park and Sunnyside in the afternoon. The trails where you'll run into the fewest people are below Sam's Knob (including Lower Powderhorn) and are designated expert, but advanced intermediates can handle them.

Aspen Mountain (Ajax). Aspen the mountain and Aspen the town go hand in hand. Both are designed for the smooth, the chic, the cool, and the expert. Yokels don't survive in Aspen for long; beginners don't survive on Ajax. Designed for fewer skiers, lift lines are shorter than at Snowmass. And while the mountain has been damned for being underdeveloped and overrated, it is praised for its unyielding commitment to slopes that will challenge the best skiers.

With good powder on the slopes, experts will feel like they're in heaven. After a heavy night's snow, the lines will begin to form at lifts 4 and 1–A at 7:00 A.M. Many report that the ultimate act of their existence is carving the first tracks on Bell Mountain Ridge for all the riders on lift 5 to see.

This lift on Bell Mountain takes you right to the peak. Although there are chutes and gullies off both sides, the Face of Bell slope is most renowned. Equally thrilling, off the #8 lift is another ridge aptly named Elevator Shaft with a handful of steep tree runs.

The variety of trails for intermediates is limited. There's Ruthie's Run, Spar Gulch, and the peak—the trails off the top of the mountain—but that's about the extent of the blue trails.

A brief word of caution: Grand Junction, at the bottom of the Spar Gulch, becomes very congested and dangerous at the end of the day.

Whatever your level, you really can't say you've skied Aspen until you've swooped down to Little Nell's at about four o'clock, clomped up to the patio, and gotten a beer and a hot dog.

THE TOWN/NIGHTLIFE

Reminders of Aspen's history as a "quaint" mining town still abound. With gracious, western-Victorian buildings lining the streets, despite the glittery reputation of the town, it can all seem rather peaceful.

But don't be deceived. Aspen has the most exciting and diverse nightlife of any ski resort in the country. There are at least one hundred good restaurants and a dozen bars catering to all tastes. Some are overrated, vastly expensive and overcrowded, but Aspen is still the place to have fun when the sun goes down.

BARS

Aspen Magazine once declared that the Best Aspen Scavenger Hunt Item was a "Happy Second Anniversary" card. It's a telling joke, and Aspen's bars and nightclubs are a playground for the single and the newly single. If you thought the Corkscrew run on Ajax required skill, wait till you try maneuvering the bars.

Fortunately, it's perfectly permissible just to sit back and watch the pros in action, wooing potential mates with tales of their latest movie, book, or drug deals. Eavesdropping is the locals' favorite pastime, and it's certainly one of the few cheap thrills in town.

And you'll find the main action after skiing at Little Nell's and The Tippler, both at the bottom of Ajax. We think Little Nell's is possibly the greatest bar in the world. From 3:00 to 5:00 on a good ski day it's filled with tanned, healthy, happy people. They can get pretty rowdy but it's a rowdiness born of total exuberance, so it's rarely destructive. The Tippler, on the other hand, is much more sedate and attracts an older crowd. A typical scenario is the thirty-five-year-old man who downs a beer at Little Nell's while ogling the ski bunnies, then heads to the Tippler where he meets his wife.

But when you ask, "What's the hottest bar in Aspen?" you hear "André's." It's hard to figure, because in any other city, André's would be a typical, sleazy fern bar. Namedropping abounds and the odor of musk and hairspray is stifling. The music is tasteless 1984-style disco, accompanied by flashing lights. But like it or not, André's is where the rich and famous come to drink and dance, and the place *is* hot, especially on the weekends.

Some of the rich and famous, however, do have some taste, and they head for Paragon, the other major hot spot in town. While it is also slightly ferny, the lighting isn't nearly as oppressive as that of André's. Its style and relaxing Victorian feel attract both skiers and locals. You'll find the Main Bar with a dance floor the focal point, but there's also a quieter room, the Parlour, that usually has a guitarist.

For an unusual and classy touch, try the "swim-up" bar at the Spinnaker, a new bar. Paddy Bugatti's also has a swim-up bar, but it's not nearly so classy. The thing that brings people to Paddy's is the diverse bands that play in its tiny lounge—everything from mellow to punk. Long an Aspen landmark, the Jerome Bar in the Hotel Jerome has been undergoing remodeling and it's hard to say if the bar will retain its flavor (the Jerome is Jack Nicholson's favorite watering hole, by the way). The Red Onion used to be the most popular local bar, but tried to go chic a few years back and lost all its local fans. It's now under new management, and is back to being a regular bar, and a good one—no pretensions, long bar, good beer selection.

But if you've had enough of the jet set—the healthy and wealthy ski crowd—and just want to drink some cheap beers and shoot pool, then Aspen has a place for you: Galena St. East. In a town where beers run $2, there you can pick up a draft for 50 cents and pitchers for $3. It can be a tough spot. It's popular with construction workers and ski bums, but on the whole, Galena St. East is a small pocket of the real world in the middle of Shangri-La.

RESTAURANTS

This is a town where $20 dinners are the norm, but we did find some relatively cheap meals and a few that aren't but are well worth the money. The Crystal Palace may cost you $30, but it's an Aspen must. Your waiters and waitresses will serve you a very decent dinner (though nothing to write home about) and then perform a series of satiric and sometimes ribald songs and skits with delightful enthusiasm and flair. The dining room and the bar are decorated with stained glass and antique cars. You'll need reservations.

Details of Aspen's restaurants would fill another book, so we'll simply highlight those on the moderate to cheap side. If you're up for Chinese food there are Eastern Winds and Arthur's. Both are great, but Eastern Winds is friendlier and less expensive. Elegant and cool—Art Deco lends a sophisticated 1930s atmosphere to the Ritz, which has a continental menu and a popular wide bar. At the base of Little Nell's is Shlomo's Deli, a small but good and surprisingly inexpensive restaurant serving standard diner fare and bagels. Little Annie's, a favorite of locals, has barbecue and offers the famed shot-and-a-beer for $1.50. For the best Mexican food in town try La Cocina. Cooper Street Pier accommodates those who want casual fare—a burger and sandwich in their place upstairs. They also have a nicer restaurant downstairs (they've got great fries, too). Need shelter from the storm? Go to Judge Bean's, where they'll warm you up with burgers and Tex-Mex food—all drinks are two-for-one if it's raining or snowing.

LODGING

Staying in Aspen can be complicated and expensive. You'll have to make your way through a maze of packages and deals. You should contact the Aspen Resort Association and get its brochures and advice first, and then decide how much you want to pay. Prices are lowest in early December, January, and April.

If you want to be close to Ajax, you couldn't choose better than the Continental Inn, Aspen's largest lodge, the Aspen Inn, the Tipple Lodge, or the Skier's Chalet. These all cost between $60 and $100 per night. The Continental has a good deal with its dorm space, which goes for $18 to $24.

Since you don't really have to worry about distance from Ajax—you'll only be a few blocks away—you should also consider the

Christmas Inn, the Alpina Haus, the Snow Queen Lodge, and the Tyrolean Lodge. These are all moderate choices in the $40 to $60 range. Real budget options ($15 to $30) include the Copper Horse Guest House, the Endeavor Lodge, and the Little Red Ski Haus. These inns offer a lot for a little money. They're small, friendly, and always have a young crowd.

You might also want to think about staying at Snowmass Village if you're only going to ski at Snowmass. But if you're one of those people who wants it all—all four mountains and the nightlife, too—we still have to recommend staying in Aspen.

ACCESSIBILITY

Aspen is 100 miles west of Denver. Aspen Airways and Rocky Mountain Airways fly into the Aspen Airport, two miles out of town. Trailways serves Aspen by bus, and all the major car rental companies have offices at the airport. Buses run frequently from the town to Snowmass, Buttermilk, and Aspen Highlands.

LISTINGS

Aspen Skiing Company
Box 1248
Aspen, CO   81612
303-925-1220

Aspen Highlands Skiing Corporation
P.O. Box T
Aspen, CO   81612
303-925-5300

Aspen Resort Association
303 Main Street
Aspen, CO   81612
Tourist Information: 303-925-1940
Central Reservations: 303-925-9000 or toll-free 800-872-7669

LIFT TICKET

Aspen Mountain (Ajax), Snowmass, Buttermilk—$22
Aspen Highlands—$22

BARS

Little Nell's, 611 East Durant, 925-3636.
The Tippler, 535 East Dean, 925-4977.
André's, 312 South Galena, 925-6200.
Paragon, 419 Hyman Avenue Mall, 925-7499.

The Spinnaker, 600 South Spring, 925-7627.
Paddy Bugatti's, 515 South Galena, 925-1287.
The Jerome Bar, 330 East Main, 925-4649.
The Red Onion, 429 Cooper Avenue Mall, 925-6853.
Galena St. East, 450 South Galena, 925-9157.

RESTAURANTS

Crystal Palace, 300 East Hyman, 925-1455.
Eastern Winds, 529 East Cooper, 925-5160.
Arthur's, 132 West Main, 925-7931.
The Ritz, 205 South Mill, 925-1212.
Shlomo's Deli, 611 East Durant, 925-3354.
Little Annie's, 517 East Hyman, 925-1098.
La Cocina, 308 East Hopkins, 925-9714.
Cooper Street Pier, 500 East Cooper, 925-7758.
Judge Bean's, 529 East Cooper, 925-8717.

LODGING

Continental Inn, 515 South Galena, 925-1150.
Aspen Inn, 701 South Mill, 925-6300.
Tipple Lodge, 747 South Galena, 925-1116.
Skier's Chalet, 710 South Aspen, 925-2904.
Christmas Inn, 232 West Main, 925-3822.
Alpina Haus, 935 East Durant, 925-7335.
Snow Queen Lodge, 124 East Cooper, 925-8455.
Tyrolean Lodge, 200 West Main, 925-4595.
Copper Horse Guest House, 328 West Main, 925-7525.
Endeavor Lodge, 905 East Hopkins, 925-2847.
The Little Red Ski Haus, 118 East Cooper, 925-3333.

BRECKENRIDGE

You couldn't ask much more of Breckenridge, barring a passion for Aspen-like glitter. Breckenridge is made up of two twin 12,000-foot peaks with 1,150 acres of skiing, and is just seventy miles from Denver. From the ski slopes to the main avenue, there is an abounding sense of vitality, exuberance, and friendliness, and though the number of slopes and skiers have grown, the town fathers have done a remarkable job of preserving yet developing the Victorian town.

If you remember hearing about Breckenridge as ho-hum—lots of snow-bunny trails but no gusto—you heard right. Two years ago, at least. Expansion into the formerly forested valley slopes between Peaks 8 and 9 has created some very tough, excellent runs and boosted the amount of expert terrain to a muscular 51 percent.

Miners settling the valley just prior to the Civil War named the town after Vice-President John C. Breckinridge. When Breckinridge announced his support for the Confederacy, the town changed the *i* to an *e*. The gold rush lured the early settlers but didn't last long, and for decades the town barely limped along. In the mid-1950s, Breckenridge was occasionally listed as a Colorado ghost town. Another kind of gold—white gold—attracted developers, and the ski resort was born. Breckenridge can be seen as a less upscale, less commercialized Aspen. Today Breckenridge and nearby Frisco are home to several thousand people. The furs, Cadillacs, and foreign languages are up over Vail Pass, but if you can live without those things, Breckenridge can't be beat.

THE SKIING

Breckenridge had the reputation of being the cream puff of Colorado skiing—plenty of easy trails and not much else. Two years ago they added the E lift to Peak 9, and experts can now be challenged by this steep, north-facing slope. And as the lines pile up at the #4 chair, you only have to wait two minutes maximum at the base of the E.

Each of Breckenridge's two mountains has its own lodge and system of trails, and most of the easy and intermediate slopes are on the sunny, front faces. Lehman and Park Lane are typical of the wide, well-groomed beginner slopes. Bonanza and American on Peak 9, and Pathfinder and Northstar on 8 are continually groomed intermediate runs, to name just a few. Eight advanced (single black diamond) trails on the front sides will be good for intermediate skiers, though true experts may be a bit bored.

From Maggie (at the base of Peak 9), the fastest way to the peak is via the A1 chair, otherwise known as the 'quad.' It has a capacity of 2,200 skiers per hour. You ski from the top of the quad to the B chair, which takes you up top. To get to the expert skiing on the valley faces between Peaks 8 and 9, take chairs 1 and 5 from the base of Peak 8. You'll probably have to wait, but they do provide the most direct route.

Chair 6 on Peak 8 serves the "back bowls" of Breckenridge. All trails there, except for Steep, are marked as black diamonds, although adventuresome intermediates won't find the trails impossible. Snow in the back bowls can get windblown and uneven, adding surprise to the upper regions.

The 51 percent expert trails we mentioned at Breckenridge aren't just hype. Many of the trails are marked with imposing double diamond signs. You can get to these slopes on E and 4 chairs, but for the most skiing, stick with E chair. Tom's Baby will take you down the area's steepest section, and Devil's Crotch is notable for its narrowness—eastern skiers will feel at home on this one.

Unless you're staying near or parked at Peak 8, at the end of the day shoot for the Peak 9 base: several happy-hour hot spots are within walking distance. And as its name implies, the Four O'Clock run will take you right into town.

THE TOWN/NIGHTLIFE

Unspoiled Breckenridge has no pretensions and no lack of good nightspots or restaurants, though there is a scant selection of inexpensive restaurants. You could cut costs by staying in a condominium and cooking, or heading into Frisco for the Pizza Hut, Taco Bell, or Kentucky Fried. But then you'd miss the choices in Breckenridge.

For just drinking start the happy hour at Mi Casa—free nachos and $5 liters of fantastic margaritas. The locals discovered this long ago. Daddy John's next door features live rock entertainment with two levels of dancing. Next to the skating pond is Flipside, a disco. It has flashing lights on the floor but is dark everywhere else. Crowded and warm, it charges no cover. The crowd is young and energetic.

The bar at the Gold Pan Restaurant makes no attempt to be high class. They don't serve beer only in pitchers, but they might as well.

The Mogul and Shamus O'Toole's Roadhouse Saloon are two other nightspots that charge a cover. The Mogul is small and lively. Shamus O'Toole's features live entertainment and may draw some of the same characters as its next-door neighbor, the Gold Pan Bar. And for the local favorite—country-western music and dancing—try the lounge at Whitney's Steakhouse, 9:00 P.M. until closing.

Fatty's is the oldest pizzeria in town and features Sicilian deep-dish pizzas and delicious pasta. Prices range from $4 to $14, and they'll serve you until 11:30 P.M. The St. Bernard on Main Street prepares northern Italian cuisine, and you can expect to pay $15 for dinner. Mi Casa and El Perdido vie for first place in Mexican fare. Mi Casa offers free quesadillas and nachos during happy hour, and El Perdido features authentic central Mexico cuisine. Both are moderately priced at around $8 per person for dinner.

In an atmosphere of nautical decor, the Whale's Tail on Main will serve you sea fare: crab, lobster, and trout. Dinners range from $9 to $20. Try the 10-cent shrimp during happy hour on weekdays. For those who hanker for a western-size steak, how does a 36-ounce porterhouse at Whitney's Steak House sound? The 8-ounce "Kit Carson" is for smaller appetites, and they also have game specialties. You can expect, on average, to pay $12 for dinner.

Locals choose the Horseshoe II Restaurant and the Blue Front Café. Both offer breakfast, lunch, and dinner in a casual atmosphere and at moderate prices. The pancakes at the Blue Front are terrific, as are the generous dinner entrees of chicken and stir-fried vegetables at the Horseshoe. You can find fondue at the 9600 Foot Club, in the village at the base of Peak 9, and delicious food at a moderate price of $6 at most.

LODGING

Over 90 percent of the beds in Breckenridge are handled through the resort's Chamber of Commerce. One toll-free call to the Breckenridge Resort Chamber will reserve lodging as well as handle your transportation needs. Beaver Run and the village of Breckenridge are two of the nicest spots. They are both just a few years old, and are located right on the mountain—Beaver Run takes you directly onto D chair, and from the village hop onto the new quad chair at Maggie Base. Beaver Run, the larger and more elegant of the two (with *six* outdoor hot tubs, for starters), will run you $90 for a double, but the Village, at $115 per room, is more convenient to town.

There are several hotels and lodges in the area as well. The Nordic Inn's dormitory-style rooms are not exceptional, but very clean and pleasant, and a bargain at $33 for a single. The Breckenridge Inn and Resort, $60 for a double, is a place the locals might recommend. For cut-rate lodging at cut-rate prices try Crofutts Nap Sack Lodge at $15 a night. At the same price, the Fireside Inn offers mostly dorm-style rooms, but one private room is available. It's very friendly and relaxed. Registered with the American Youth Hostel, the Fireside provides meals on a sign-up basis at an extra charge, and it has a hot tub, too. The Fireside is a good ten-minute walk from the slopes.

For a big, full-service hotel there's the Best Western Lake Dillon Lodge right off I–70. It's not really convenient to Breckenridge, but it's a good location for skiing all of the Summit County areas—Copper Mountain and Keystone. Singles cost $68, doubles $80.

Condominiums are the most popular type of lodging, and differences arise in the amenities: shuttle bus, swimming pool, Jacuzzi, phones in the rooms, laundry facilities, etc. Price is also a consideration, ranging from $165 a night for one bedroom at Beaver Run to $60 a night at the Motherlode.

For more of an escape, several homes are available, but are reasonable only for large groups of 8 to 12.

ACCESSIBILITY

Breckenridge is eighty-six miles west of Denver. Trailways runs from Denver's Stapleton Airport to Frisco, ten miles away, and there are shuttles from Frisco to the ski area.

LISTINGS

Breckenridge Ski Area
Box 1058
Breckenridge, CO   80424
303–453–2918
800–221–1091

Summit County Chamber of Commerce
60 Summit City Road
Fraser, CO   80424
303–668–5800

LIFT TICKET

$20

RESTAURANTS

Fatty's, 106 North Ridge Street, 453–9802.
St. Bernard, 103 South Main, 453–2572.
Mi Casa, 600 Park Avenue, 453–2071.
El Perdido, 306 North French, 453–2928.
Whale's Tail, 323 South Main, 453–2221.
Whitney's Steak House, 130 South Ridge, 453–1733.
Horseshoe II Restaurant, 115 Main, 453–9804.
Blue Front Cafe, 1953 Blazing Saddles Center, 453–1357.
9600 Foot Club, 450 South Columbine, 453–6759.

BARS

Mogul, 109 South Main, 453–0999.
Shamus O'Toole's Roadside Saloon, 115 South Ridge, 453–2004.
Flipside, 655 South Park, 453–6600.
Gold Pan Restaurant, 105 North Main, 453–9075.

Mi Casa, 600 Park Avenue, 453–2071.

LODGING

Beaver Run, 649 Village Road, 453–6000 or toll-free 800–525–2253.

The Village at Breckenridge, Bell Tower Mall, 453–9985 or toll-free 800–321–8552.

Nordic Inn, 205 South French, 453–9985.

Breckenridge Inn, 600 South Ridge, 453–2333 or from Denver dial direct 892–1934.

Crofutts Nap Sack Lodge, 200 Ski Hill Road, 453–2460.

Fireside Inn, 114 French, 453–6456.

Best Western Lake Dillon Lodge, Exit 203 off I-70, 668–5094 or toll-free 800–528–1234.

COPPER MOUNTAIN

Probably best described by comparing it to its neighbors, Copper Mountain is a kind of a mini-Vail, rather chic and exclusive, but without the cutesy village and the crowds. It's also kind of a mini-Keystone—very modern, fairly expensive, but without Ralston-Purina's money for large expansion. Copper seems happy to remain a rather small, beautiful, and tranquil little ski area, and while, because of the cost, it's probably not the best choice for readers of this book, the resort does offer a fine mountain and a peaceful vacation.

There is a Club Med there, but don't expect that to liven things up. Club Med has an entirely separate "compound" in the village, and doesn't really mix with the rest of the vacationers at the mountain. So if you're looking for a wild Jacuzzi party, you'll have to find your own. You can, of course, attempt to sneak in and join them, but you'll probably get caught.

During the week Copper is quite peaceful. The resort only has about 2,500 beds, and you'll rarely have problems with crowds on weekdays. But on weekends, watch out, because Copper is a favorite

COPPER MOUNTAIN RESORT

ski area for Denver residents, being just seventy-five miles away on the interstate. Forty-five-minute lines at the base lifts are not unusual, and the few restaurants in the village are jammed in the evening. But during the weekday, the resort exists mainly for serious skiers. Most people run lots and lots of trails each day, and when evening comes, a decent meal, maybe a fireplace, and a soft bed are all anyone can manage. In other words, there's no nightlife. For excitement, you might try Copper's new $2.7-million athletic complex, which has everything the fitness freak could want—an indoor swimming pool, Jacuzzis, saunas, steam baths, Nautilus equipment, racquetball and tennis courts, etc. Use of the facility costs $10 per day.

THE SKIING

The ski trails on Copper Mountain were designed in a lovely way— beginners, intermediates, and experts each have their own nearly distinct areas of the mountain—and like nearby Vail, the mountain has great balance: 30 percent novice, 40 percent intermediate, and 30 percent expert. As you move west to east, the trails gradually become more difficult.

The east side of the mountain provides the most challenging terrain for experts. Portions of Collage, Rosie's Run, and Ordeal were used in the 1984 U.S. Alpine Championships. Far East, Two Much, and Triple Threat are long and fairly tough. Oh No is probably the steepest trail on the mountain. Many of the expert runs can be handled by intermediates who are trying to work their way up to expert status. Lift lines on the east side are usually the shortest on the mountain.

As you move west, the mountain combines intermediate with advanced slopes. Union Bowl, the fifty-acre area above the treeline, is a lot of fun and accessible to all levels of skier. If you love moguls, try Union Peak, Kaboom, and Endeavor. From the top of the mountain, you'll get a truly spectacular view of the Ten Mile Range—you can even see Vail. Bouncer, Bittersweet, and Main Vein offer some attractive forested runs with enough twists to challenge. Soliloquy and Roundabout, two of the longest runs on the mountain, are favorites with beginners. Novice skiers will especially like the fact that they can ski from the top of the mountain to the bottom, all on very easy slopes.

THE TOWN/NIGHTLIFE

As noted before, people come to Copper Mountain to ski and get some peace and quiet, and nightlife is almost nil. Though a few spots draw small crowds to happy hours after the slopes close, the resort is pretty much dead after 9:00 P.M. The Center, located at the base of F and G lifts, offers live entertainment after skiing. Jacques' Loft, located on the third floor of the Center, shows your NASTAR race on

TV. The Columbine Café in the Village Square and Farley's in the Snowflake Building are the two liveliest bars at the resort. The cozy Columbine offers live music and usually attracts the ski instructors. Farley's, probably the most popular spot right after the lifts close, also has live music and a good happy hour.

If you're really looking for excitement you'll have to check out the bars in Breckenridge or Keystone, a few miles away.

There's not much choice for food, either (especially inexpensive), but the few restaurants in the village are generally good. Since the resort consists mostly of condos with full kitchen facilities, most people choose to eat in. Farley's, already mentioned as a good pub for after skiing, offers an attractive Old English atmosphere and a wide variety of entrees, with especially good prime rib. Also, don't miss Farley's warm cinnamon bread and mud pie—they're outstanding. Dinner at Farley's will run about $15 or so. Tuso's Bar and Restaurant also sports a friendly atmosphere, but it's a bit livelier and more popular than Farley's. Tuso's, with an attractive greenhouse, specializes in homemade pasta dishes and Mexican fare. It also has some great specialty drinks. The Plaza is the area's most elegant restaurant, nestled at the base of the mountain in the center of the village. Linen tablecloths and fresh flowers create a posh, romantic aura. The food is primarily steaks and chicken, and it's good but a bit overpriced at $20 or so. Be prepared for a long, long dinner at Mike and Miquel's— the service is slow, the food is mediocre and expensive (about $15). The Columbine Café, probably the cheapest place in town for a nice dinner, serves international dishes in a casual setting. You can get by for $7 to $10. Finally, for junk-food fans, there's B-Lift Pizza (a good lunch choice), Vlasta Pizza, and Arby's.

LODGING

Convenient, deluxe condominium units and first-class hotel accommodations are all you'll find at Copper Mountain. There's not even any dorm space. All of the lodging, including Club Med, is designed beautifully and located at the base of the mountain—all within easy walking distance of the slopes and lifts.

Five property management services manage the twenty-two condominium buildings in the village (excluding Club Med). Each condominium unit and/or hotel accommodation is equipped with all the amenities—saunas, Jacuzzis, balconies, fireplaces, pools, color TV, etc. Condos generally start in the $105 range, and hotel rooms in the $80 range. Of course, they go much higher. Package deals, especially in the off-season periods, can cut these costs quite a bit. For all reservations, contact the Copper Mountain lodging service. We've also listed the individual management companies below, in case you need more detailed information.

If you can't afford the village, then your next best alternative is one of the motels in Frisco or Dillon, a few miles east. You'll need a car to get to the mountain, however, since Copper's free shuttle operates only in the Village and between the base areas of Keystone, Breckenridge, and Arapahoe Basin.

ACCESSIBILITY

Copper Mountain, in Summit County, is seventy-five miles west of Denver and seventeen miles east of Vail, right off Interstate 70. Trailways and American Limousine (twelve-person vans) provide daily service from Denver's airport to the resort.

LISTINGS

Copper Mountain Resort
Copper Mountain, CO   80443
303-968-6477
Lodging: 303-968-2882 or toll-free 800-525-3891

LIFT TICKET

$21

RESTAURANTS AND NIGHTLIFE

Jacques' Loft, in The Center, 968-2882, ext. 6515.
Columbine Café, 189 Ten Mile Circle, 968-2156.
Farley's Restaurant, 104 Wheeler Place, 968-2577.
Tuso's Bar and Restaurant, Snowflake Building, 968-6090.
The Plaza Restaurant, 209 Ten Mile Circle, 968-6000.
Mike and Miquel's, 760 Copper Road, 968-6841.
B-Lift Pizza, Snowflake Building, 968-2525.
Vlasta Pizza, 760 Copper Road, 968-2323.
Arby's, 230 Ten Mile Circle, 968-2596.

LODGING

The Copper Mountain lodging service also handles all reservations for the companies below:
Carbonate Property Management, 35 Wheeler Place, 968-6854.
The Foxpine Inn Management Company, 154 Wheeler Place, 968-2600.
Resort Properties Management, P.O. Box 3356, 968-2626.
Rocky Mountain Property Management, P.O. Box 3280, 968-6840 or toll-free 800-525-3887.

CRESTED BUTTE

Combining the slopes of Purgatory and the charm of Telluride's town, Crested Butte is a great place to ski. Many think of it as an old friend; nothing really outrageous or flashy, just nice and reliable.

Located thirty miles north of Gunnison, Crested Butte is fairly remote, but not as much so as Telluride. A heated battle over expansion in the early seventies gave way to the construction of a series of expensive and boring condos at the base of the mountain, a $40-million convention facility currently under construction, and a charmingly antique town three miles from the slopes. Crested Butte isn't out to attract the mogul maniacs, the super-experts, or the glitterati. It's happy to cater to church and college groups and to young professionals on vacation. The pace is delightfully relaxed and friendly.

THE SKIING

Crested Butte's slopes are great for cruisers and bombers, but a bit short on vertical feet.

Crested Butte is a delight for beginners and intermediates. Experts will get bored. Hope that the Outer Limits will be open, or they could

learn telemarking, both of which we'll discuss later. Novice skiers have three lifts all to themselves. Peachtree and Painter Boy are the easiest and have four fine, wide, undemanding runs to explore—great for building confidence in turning technique. The trails off the Keystone lift are harder, and if you're a beginner and you make it all the way down Roller Coaster and Lower Keystone without falling you should feel proud of yourself.

Cascade and Panion's, off the Gold Link lift, are just challenging enough to build confidence in the advanced beginner.

Intermediates will have their fun with the great long runs off the top of the Paradise lift. Ruby Chief down to the bottom of Red Lady, or the full Treasury run are nearly two exhilarating miles. The way they alternate between speedy straightaways and mini-mogul fields will really challenge the skill and endurance of any intermediate.

Experts will find Resurrection and Crystal enjoyable, but even the longest black trail, International, is better suited for the advanced intermediate. The real challenge for experts at Crested Butte lies off the trails in the Outer Limits. Renowned for deep powder and terrifying drops, these bowls and slopes are open only a few weeks each season. Tough hiking is necessary on all runs, and on some you may need a guide. Use caution when skiing these trails. A skier was killed by an avalanche on Banana when he ignored the fact that the trail was officially closed.

Crested Butte is known as the leader in telemark skiing—a mixture of cross-country and downhill. Telemarking is both exhausting and difficult to master, but it's a lovely sight when done well, as you will see at Crested Butte. Many expert skiers who become bored with even the most demanding trails now see telemarking as a new challenge. In addition to fine downhill instructors, Crested Butte offers some of the best telemarking teachers in the country.

THE TOWNS

Crested Butte, the real town, and Mount Crested Butte, the new ski village, coexist three miles apart. (They are connected by a free shuttle bus.) The ski village is fairly standard, and you won't find anything out of the ordinary about its restaurants or atmosphere. There is Rafters, the bar above the main base building, and it's a fun spot for a beer or two after skiing. Occasionally some good bands play there.

Like Moses, you have to go down the mountain to catch the action. Crested Butte's diverse collection of fine restaurants, burger joints, and Old West saloons will not disappoint.

Although the town has a population of 1,200, you can actually get as much exercise barhopping as skiing. The bar downstairs at Talk of the Town is popular and often attracts some first-class rock bands. Kochevar's has suffered a decline in popularity recently, but we think it's the second-best bar in town. With its unpretentious atmosphere, pool tables, darts, beat-up bar and fascinating antiques, it has the distinction of serving Watney's ale and Heineken on tap.

But without a doubt, the Wooden Nickel, Crested Butte's oldest saloon, scores as number one. It's hard to pin down, but the Nickel is perhaps the warmest, most comfortable bar we visited in Colorado. It's the kind of place where even locals and ski management drink side by side.

While you could dine at Penelope's, a charming Victorian-style spot, we recommend it for breakfast. Sitting in the greenhouse in the back with the morning light pouring in is enchanting and invigorating. We also recommend the Forest Queen, a quaint hotel near the end of Elk Avenue, for breakfast.

Acknowledged as the best restaurant in town, the tiny Soupçon requires reservations days in advance. Despite the price tag of $25 or so for the French cuisine, you'll agree it's a deal. Le Bosquet is a larger, slightly cheaper rival of Soupçon.

On Thursdays, you must make an appearance at the famous Margarita Night at the Elk Mountain Lodge. Cheap, potent pitchers are $4, and at least half the crowd ends up south of the border. The Elk Mountain serves rather good Mexican food, but it's a bit expensive.

Grubsteak is another must. It claims to have the largest liquor selection in Colorado, and we don't doubt it. Happy hours are from 4:00 to 6:30 and again from 10:00 to midnight, and while you're there try the prime rib, cooked slowly in rock salt. It's perfection.

A bit off the beaten track, Slogar's is another ornate Victorian restaurant. It's slightly chichi, but still appealing. The Gourmet Noodle has simpler fare—homemade noodles. For burgers, try Talk of the Town (but avoid their Chinese food).

LODGING

While the condos and lodges at Mount Crested Butte are all quite nice and well appointed, their prices are not so accommodating. Fortunately, they drop in proportion to their distance from the base. You will pay a king's ransom to stay at the Crested Butte Lodge, the Columbine or Butte's Condos, a smaller fortune at the Mountain Sunrise, Outrun, Eagle's Nest, or Chateau Condos.

If you don't mind a short drive or bus ride, we suggest you stay in town. It's a lot more fun and lodging can be significantly cheaper. There are a number of possibilities: for $30 a night, the Four Seasons provides you with a bed, a big breakfast, and free use of the spa next door—the only public spa in town. Often the hot water in the Jacuzzi provides only half the steam. Rozman's is a large motel, and the Ore Bucket Lodge specializes in church groups. Both the Elk Mountain Lodge ($25 to $40) and the Forest Queen Hotel ($12 to $30) are well-established former boardinghouses for miners. The Purple Mountain

Lodge ($32 to $40) is a classic ski lodge, but a bit far from the action in town.

ACCESSIBILITY

Crested Butte is 230 miles southwest of Denver and 30 miles north of Gunnison. Frontier Airlines and Trans-Colorado Airlines fly into Gunnison, and there's shuttle service from the airport to the mountain. Also, you can fly into Montrose, 96 miles away, on Delta, Frontier, and Trans-Colorado. Continental Trailways provides bus service to Gunnison. To get between Crested Butte and Mount Crested Butte, use the free shuttle that operates from 7:00 A.M. to midnight.

LISTINGS

Crested Butte Mountain Resort
Box A
Mount Crested Butte, CO   81225
303–349–2333 (in Colorado)
800–525–4220 (toll-free)

Crested Butte Chamber of Commerce
Box 1288
Old Town Hall
Crested Butte, CO   81224
303–349–6438

LIFT TICKET

$19

BARS

Kochevar's, 127 Elk Avenue, 349–6745.
The Wooden Nickel, 222 Elk Avenue, 349–9983.

RESTAURANTS

Rafters, in the base lodge at the mountain, 349–2249.
Soupçon, 127A Elk Avenue (behind The Forest Queen), 349–5448.
Le Bosquet, Second and Elk Avenues, 349–5808.
Penelope's, 120 Elk Avenue, 349–5178.
The Forest Queen, 129 Elk Avenue, 349–5336.
The Elk Mountain Lodge, Second and Gothic, 349–6674.
Grubsteak, 229 Elk Avenue, 349–6107.
Slogar, 517 Second Avenue, 349–5765.
The Gourmet Noodle, 411 Third Street, 349–7401.
Talk of the Town, 230 Elk Avenue, 349–6809.

LODGING

Crested Butte Lodge, Mount Crested Butte, 349–5322.

The Columbine, Mount Crested Butte, 349–2451.

Butte's Condos, Mount Crested Butte, 349–5322.

Mountain Sunrise Condos, Mount Crested Butte, 349–6629.

The Outrun, Mount Crested Butte, 349–2800.

Eagle's Nest, Mount Crested Butte, 349–7131.

Chateaux Condos, Mount Crested Butte, 349–2500.

The Four Seasons, 32 Elk Avenue, 349–7331.

Rozman's, Highway 135 and Whiterock Avenue, 349–6669.

The Ore Bucket Lodge, 621 Maroon Avenue, 349–5519.

The Elk Mountain Lodge, 129 Gothic Avenue, 349–5114.

The Forest Queen Hotel, 129 Elk Avenue, 349–5336.

KEYSTONE/
ARAPAHOE BASIN

Good words to remember about Keystone/Arapahoe Basin are convenience, service, intermediate skiing, and Ralston-Purina. Owned entirely by the company famous for animal chow, Keystone resort is best described as a planned, family-oriented vacation resort. Keystone is designed with the ski vacationer in mind and all the courteous employees—from the grocer to the restaurant busboys—wear the same orange name pins. Instead of the usual ski bums, most employees are farm kids from the midwest. Ralston-Purina is finicky about its employees, and most visitors will notice the uniformly friendly and helpful attitude of Keystone workers.

Despite Keystone's careful supervision, a certain feeling of mountain community is lacking from the resort. Everything is *so* planned and new that any sense of "Skitown USA" becomes lost between gourmet meals at the Ranch and the shops at Keystone Village. Like

Vail, there's a Disneyesque aura to the place—planned and polished. Many skiers love this combination, though, and Keystone's packages can make the area even more attractive.

Most visitors find the best way to enjoy Keystone is just to stay put and savor the consistently fine services. Clustered around a central area in Keystone Village, all of the shops and restaurants are close to many of the rental condominiums and the Keystone Lodge. You may be put off by the newness and corporate flavor, but the resort offers many amenities not found in other areas. The lodge and condominiums are among the nicest around. For example, the central sports desk coordinates such varied activities as snowcat tours, sleigh rides, and hot-air balloon rides.

Further, construction began last May on an ambitious, $15-million expansion program that is scheduled to be completed in November, 1984. A third mountain, North Peak, will be developed with a gondola, three new lifts, and fifteen trails, thus increasing the total ski capacity by 58 percent. According to the resort management, the new terrain will be primarily expert and advanced intermediate. Also, a posh new mountain village a half-mile from the existing complex is scheduled for completion in mid-November.

Though not for everyone, Keystone could be just the spot if you want a complete ski vacation at an intermediate area.

THE SKIING

Keystone is made up of two mountains: Keystone, with 70 percent beginner-intermediate terrain, and Arapahoe Basin, five miles up the Loveland Pass road, which has the very steep and famous Pallavicini run. One lift ticket allows you to ski both areas, and a free shuttle will take you back and forth. Even though Keystone is a popular mountain, lift lines are rare on the upper lifts, and only reach fifteen minutes at worst on the bottom lifts.

Looking at Keystone from the base of the mountain, you wonder where the 440 acres of skiing are. Rather than come crashing down from a great height, the trails on Keystone descend gently from a summit elevation of 11,640. You must actually ski the mountain to get a good look at the wide and well-groomed slopes.

Since Keystone only has 30 percent expert trails, advanced skiers may decide to spend more time at Arapahoe Basin. But many people find that Keystone trails like Wild Irishman, Paymaster, and School-marm provide plenty of thrills. Most trails are frequently groomed; only a few slopes are allowed to grow moguls. So it's hard not to ski well here. Much of the area is serviced by snowmaking as well, guaranteeing good conditions in lean seasons—a key item when planning a vacation in advance.

Five miles is all the distance between Keystone and Arapahoe—but there's a world of difference in the skiing. Arapahoe is smaller and steeper, with a fair amount of above-timberline trails. On a predominantly expert mountain there are even trails for beginners—descending from the 12,450-foot summit, Dercum's Gulch. From mid-mountain, the beginner has more options, with most trails taking a wide swing around the steep trails under the lifts.

There is good reason for expert skiers' love of Arapahoe Basin. The Pallavicini lift in particular leads to steep, often mogul-filled runs. Skiing the almost endless variety of routes down is a thrill—gullies, shoots, and super-steep sections abound. You won't get bored on the Pallavicini lift—just deliciously exhausted.

THE TOWN/NIGHTLIFE

Keystone after dark is quiet. It's a family resort and locals tend to provide the only excitment. There are a few nightclubs and bars, but they either lack exuberance or are packed with locals.

You'll have to pay a small cover for live rock entertainment at the Last Chance Saloon. They have the largest dance floor in Summit County and it's usually quite crowded. For a lively time, head up the road toward Arapahoe Basin to the Snake River Saloon, which has a restaurant and bar. Its saloon is the hottest place around, and the cover is only $2. Go back down the road to the flashing neon "Bar" sign and you'll be at the Old Dillon Inn, a friendly local watering hole. Always packed by 7:00 with drinkers and Mexican food fans, the Dillon has a $2 cover Friday through Sunday for live entertainment.

Or enjoy a peaceful evening sipping drinks and nibbling gorp before a roaring fire on the fourth floor of the Keystone Lodge. Again, a wild nightlife is not the major attraction here—the prospect of a trouble-free, relaxing vacation is.

Among the off-slope activities available is ice skating on the lake. Visitors pay $2, and skate rentals are another $2. As mentioned, the sports desk handles reservations for snowmobiling and snowcat tours to the top of Keystone Mountain, and ballooning. The highlight of evening travel rides is dinner served at the restored Soda Creek Homestead. This can be arranged through the central sports desk.

There's even something for tennis fans—the John Gardiner Tennis Center has two indoor courts. And cross-country ski lessons, rentals, and access to miles of trails are available at the Cross Country Center, operated by Jana Hlavaty, former Olympic nordic competitor. On your own you can explore several creeks further up the Montezuma Road. Peru Creek, for one, leads up to the Pennsylvania Mine, long abandoned but with some of the old structures and equipment waiting to be investigated.

89

RESTAURANTS

Right off the fourth floor of the Keystone Lodge are two excellent restaurants—the Garden Room and the Bighorn Room. Dine on continental fare in a friendly atmosphere full of greenery at the Garden Room. Reservations are recommended; meals cost about $18. Next door, the Bighorn Room offers Rocky Mountain trout as well as steak. More suitable for families, meals here run between $12 and $15.

If you want to eat with a view of the ice skaters, go to the Brasserie. Open at 6:30 A.M., it serves huge, delicious sandwiches at lunch and Italian dishes in the evening. Surprisingly, the Brasserie is relatively inexpensive ($5 to $10) and more casual than other Keystone restaurants. Chart you course for seafood at the Navigator on the other side of the lake. Clam chowder and a thirty-item salad bar are included in the dinner price of about $15 to $18. Enjoy Maine lobster and fifty-cent oysters while a piano bar plays light music.

For more flash, try Bentley's, which has an Art Deco interior and features hearty sandwiches, a giant TV screen, and a nice bar. Dinners are in the $4 to $6 range. Bentley's is solace for homesick New Yorkers. Keystone's Mexican restaurant, the Cadillac, offers chimichangas, chilis rellenos, and tamales. Its salsa has more bite than you'd expect. Have a margarita at the two-for-one drinks special from 4 to 6 P.M., or choose from Bentley's selection of beers while nibbling its great nachos.

If price is no consideration, sit down to a five-course, thoroughly western, elegant meal at the Ranch. Reservations are required at this fifty-year-old homestead, and the menu changes daily.

All of the aforementioned are Keystone-operated. The independent Alf's Gasthof Bavaria is an established, authentic German restaurant whose menu includes knockwurst and goulash. Dinner costs about $14, and Alf's is open for breakfast and lunch as well. Get to Pezzini's Chocolate Haus before 8:00 P.M. on weekends and sample their sodas, sandwiches, and chocolate.

LODGING

The philosophy behind accommodations at Keystone is convenience—not variety. Of the 900 condominiums, most are privately owned, and the lodges are under the management of the Ralston-Purina Company, as is the one first-class hotel, the Keystone Lodge. Ranging in size from studios to four-bedroom units, all condominiums have access to a pool, sauna, and Jacuzzi. And because of strict furnishing requirements, you can expect each to be well-appointed. (They also receive daily housekeeping service.)

If space for eight isn't sufficient, a limited number of private homes are available. For a group of ten or more, such rental is very reasonable. And the bus service to the slopes is within walking distance of the front porch in most cases.

The Keystone Lodge offers the finest in service—valet parking, bus service directly to Arapahoe Basin and Keystone, fine restaurants, and close proximity to a variety of specialty shops. Regular season rates for double occupancy range from $98 to $106 per night. If you're interested in a complete vacation, the Keystone is ideal—all the frills are considered basics here.

Colorado's oldest guest ranch, the Ski Tip, was recently acquired by Ralston-Purina, but this secluded, rustic, and romantic ranch has retained the same management. Free of the customary glitter, the ranch provides a hearty breakfast and dinner served family-style, and you can relax away from the blare of television while still having easy access to the telephone. The new Cross Country Center is across the clearing, with thirty-three kilometers of trails available. If you appreciate mountain serenity and cozy accommodations, the Ski Tip is well worth consideration. It costs a bit, though: $50 for dorm rooms, $90 for a single, and $115 for a double.

Independently owned lodging does exist in the Keystone area. For instance, the Tenderfoot Motel along the highway on the way to Arapahoe Basin has cabins or motel rooms. Without any amenities, they are a bargain at $40 for a double, and $67 for a larger cabin sleeping five. The Super 8 Motel, in Dillon, is popular with midwestern college students. It's easy to guess why—singles are $39, doubles $44, and it's very friendly.

ACCESSIBILITY

Keystone is just seventy miles from Denver. Buses run several times daily to the resort from Denver's airport.

LISTINGS

Keystone Resort
Box 38
Keystone, CO   80435
General information: 303–468–2316
Reservations only: 303–468–4242.

LIFT TICKET

$21

NIGHTLIFE

Last Chance Saloon, Keystone Resort, 468–4185.
Snake River Saloon, 23074 U.S. Highway 6, 468–2788.
Old Dillon Inn, 305 Dillon Lane in Silverthorne, 468–2791.

RESTAURANTS

The Keystone Ranch (at the golf course), 468–4161.

Alf's Gasthof Bavaria, 22954 U.S. Highway 6, 468–2702.

Pezzini's Chocolate Haus, 468–6898.

The following are all located at the Keystone Village:

The Garden Room, 468–2316.

Bighorn Room, 468–2316.

The Brasserie, 468–4127.

The Navigator, 468–5600.

Bentley's, 468–6610.

Cadillac Restaurant, 468–4205.

LODGING

Keystone Lodge, Keystone Resort, 468–4242.

Keystone Condominiums, Keystone Resort, 468–4242.

Ski Tip Ranch, Montezuma Road, 468–9928.

Tenderfoot Lodge, 22784 U.S. Highway 6, 468–2254.

Super 8 Motel, 808 Little Beaver Trail, Dillon, 468–8888.

PURGATORY

"Comin' on Strong" . . . Purgatory's ungrammatical motto is pretty much on target. Formerly skied primarily by Durango residents, this area is building a reputation as a solid, well-rounded resort. With a $250-million (yes, $250,000,000) expansion plan well underway, people are saying Purgatory could become a premier ski area by 1990.

It's a family mountain—good for beginners, great for intermediates, but ultimately disappointing for experts.

But so what? The majority of skiers fall into the advanced beginner/intermediate range anyway, so Purgatory will be satisfying for most. The climate is generally good, you can count on snow, and the lift lines are short. What more could you ask?

Well, it would be great if they could move Durango about twenty-five miles north. If Taos is the combination of a pueblo and a McDonald's, then Durango is the combination of an Old West saloon and a Holiday Inn.

But once you get past the neon lights of the motels and fast-food joints on the main road and enter the restored heart of town, you're in a marvelous throwback to the Gay Nineties, complete with Victorian restaurants, quaint shops, elegant hotels, and some very boisterous saloons.

THE SKIING

You'll find it hard to get lost on Purgatory's trails—they're extremely well marked with big, bright, easy-to-follow signs. You won't find yourself suddenly teetering on the brink of a black diamond.

There is even a separate lift and ski area for novices. A good place to learn, the lift #7 run is far from the intimidating crowd. Most beginners will tire of this area in a few hours, and, fortunately, there are enjoyable green runs off every lift except #5. (Damifino, the novice trail off #5, is irritatingly flat and better skied with cross-country equipment.)

The intermediate slopes are diverse, though perhaps a little too flat. There are bumps on Tinker's Dam and the lower parts of Boogie, but on the whole the intermediate runs do not really prepare you for expert moguls. They are, however, great for bombers.

Skiing Limbo to Demon fast can be wild if speed turns you on, and the lower part of Demon, where a challenging gully keeps you always just off balance, is a blast. Dead Spike and Zinfandel are also solid blues, and the views from Zinfandel are lovely.

There are only four major runs for the expert at Purgatory—Styx, Snag, Wapati, and Bull Run. The most famous is Styx, but even it lacks the vertical feet necessary to give you that heart-in-the-throat feeling experts so crave.

Purgatory provides one of the best programs for handicapped skiers in the country, and is committed to it, as well as to attracting more and more student groups with special group deals and fun weekends, like the famous Snowdown winter carnival in January.

THE TOWN

Durango is a cool town with an infectious spirit of fun and western hijinks—a lot western and a little bit country. Even if you stay on the strip of motels on Highway 550, don't cheat yourself by not exploring the refurbished Old West section in the heart of town. Even the McDonald's, located right next to the gorgeous old narrow-gauge railroad, has a distinct western flavor.

As for nightlife, only Aspen can rival Durango in sheer number of good bars.

To many, the Sundance *is* Durango. Though it appeals to an over-thirty crowd, most everyone goes there to kick up their heels to a live country-western band. Five old gents in a photo on the back wall gaze stoically on the citizens of Durango, in Levis and baseball caps, out for a big night on the town.

The younger crowd heads for Farquahrts—the only real rock 'n' roll joint in Durango (try the pizza). There is also a disco at the Holiday Inn, but that doesn't really count. Every Holiday Inn west of New Jersey has a disco.

If you're in that in-between age group, the Sixth Street Parlor may be just right for you. The rock is mellower but still good, and it attracts a sociable crowd.

If you're looking for smoke-filled rooms, pool tables, and the like, El Rancho and the Gold Slipper may be just right, but El Rancho wins on sheer toughness . . . ranch hands in flannel shirts and their women come in to play pool, drink cheap beer, and fight. The Gold Slipper, Durango's oldest saloon, is a little more sedate but still pretty tough. Neither bar depends on skiers to survive.

If you want to hang out with the ski set, go to the Crystal Tavern and the Solid Muldoon. Both are mellow. The Crystal Tavern is more western than the Muldoon, where you may want to sink into one of the sofas.

For our money, though, the Diamond Belle is the place to drink. In the historic Strater Hotel, you'll find this Gay Nineties saloon, complete with a ragtime piano player and waitresses in cancan outfits, straight out of any grade-B western. You half-expect Miss Kitty and the sheriff to come through the doors at any minute. Though the

Diamond Belle is a bit too classy for a real showdown, the place is great, and many consider the margaritas there the best in town.

By the way, up at the ski area two decent bars serve those just off the slopes. There's Purgy's, the old standard, casual and friendly, and Sterling's, new and sophisticated, which gets the older crowd.

It's easy to recommend the handful of good restaurants, but they are rather expensive. The Palace and the Ore House are especially noteworthy. (Locals voted the Palace the best restaurant in town, so who are we to quibble?) You will dine on steak and seafood in a plush Victorian interior, and even though it will cost you $15 or so, it's a good deal. Though more informal, the Ore House is also very popular, and its rough western decor spurs people to buy rounds of beer for strangers at neighboring tables. The Ore House specializes in steak and lobster, and its salad bar is overwhelming. You may overhear conversations about softball, which is even more popular than skiing in Durango.

The Eye of the Eagle, a fairly new spot, is getting great reviews for its elegance and simple, classic menu. For excellent seafood go to the Lost Pelican. You'll find good Mexican dishes at both Francisco's and Dos Juans. Of all the restaurants mentioned so far, the New York Bakery is the least expensive—and it's also great for breakfast and lunch (just try to finish the French toast!). There's a branch in the Village Center at Purgatory, too. Back to baseball, the Durango Diner, a no-frills coffee shop, has an impressive collection of baseball caps, and serves good diner fare as well as being the locals' lunch favorite.

LODGING

As part of Purgatory's expansion, some lovely condos have been built recently at the base of the mountain. If you can afford it, stay there or up the road a mile at Cascade Village. Cascade's accurate slogan is "Simply the Finest."

Coming off the mountain, there are scads of motels lining Highway 550. Most offer HBO, Jacuzzis, saunas, free ski shuttle, etc., and are priced between $25 and $50. You won't find much difference between the Gypsy Motel, the Edelweiss, the Frontier, the Landmark, or the two dozen others, so shop around at three or four for the best deal.

The lodgings in the heart of town are different, though. If you can afford it, stay at either the Strater or the General Palmer House, two charming, turn-of-the-century hotels with great canopied beds and antiques in the rooms. The Strater is really nicer, but both are in the $40 to $70 range. The Travelodge won't offer any surprises. There are two hostels as well for the truly budget-minded—the Durango Hostel and the Central Hostel and Hotel. At $9.25 per night, the Durango Hotel is cheaper ($7.25 for AYH members) than the Central (starting at $20 per night), but the Central offers private rooms with shared bathrooms.

ACCESSIBILITY

Purgatory is 25 miles north of Durango on U.S. Highway 550, 210 miles north of Albuquerque, and 340 miles southwest of Denver. Frontier, Aspen Airways, Trans-Colorado, Mesa Air, and Sun West Airlines fly into La Plata Airport in Durango. Limousine and shuttle services are available at the airport, as are rental cars (Avis, Budget, Hertz, and National). Continental Trailways provides bus service to Durango.

LISTINGS

Purgatory/Durango Central Reservations
534 Main Avenue
Durango, CO 81301
303-247-8900 (in Colorado)
800-525-0892 (toll-free)

Durango Chamber of Commerce
P.O. Box 2587-AG
Durango, CO 81301
303-247-0314

LIFT TICKET

$19

BARS

Sundance, 601 Second Avenue, 247-8821.
Farquahrts, 725 Main Avenue, 247-5440.
Sixth Street Parlor, 110 West Sixth Street, 259-2888.
El Rancho, 975 Main Avenue, 247-9855.
The Crystal Tavern, 809 Main Avenue, 259-5781.
The Solid Muldoon, 561 Main Avenue, 247-9151.
The Diamond Belle, 699 Main Avenue, 247-4431.

RESTAURANTS

The Palace, #1 Depot Place, 247-2018.
The Ore House, 147 Sixth Street, 247-5707.
The Eye of the Eagle, Tenth Street and Main Avenue, 259-6474.
The Lost Pelican, 658 Main Avenue, 247-8502.
New York Bakery (in Durango), 750 Main Avenue, 259-1007; (at Purgatory) North Village Center, 247-9000.
Francisco's, 619 Main Avenue, 247-4098.
Dos Juans, 431 East Second Avenue, 259-0550.

LODGING

Cascade Village, 50827 Highway 550 North, 259–3500, or toll-free 800–525–0896.

The Gypsy Motel, 3701 Main Avenue, 247–9950.

The Edelweiss, 689 County Road 203, 247–5685.

The Frontier, 3131 Main Avenue, 247–5460.

The Landmark, 3030 Main Avenue, 259–1333.

The Strater, 699 Main Avenue, 247–4431.

The General Palmer House, 567 Main Avenue, 247–4747.

The Durango Hostel, 543 East Second Avenue, 247–9905.

The Central Hotel and Hostel, 975 Main Avenue, 247–0330.

STEAMBOAT SPRINGS

Don't come to Steamboat if you want thumping discos, beautiful people, and fast-lane hoopla. Don't come to Steamboat if you thrive on steep, oh-my-God moguled trails. And especially don't come to Steamboat if you depend on long lift lines in order to get your suntan.

If you're searching for first-rate intermediate skiing, virtually no lift lines, and down-home western hospitality complete with cowboy hats, "champagne" powder, and an incredibly beautiful valley, make your plans for Steamboat. It's one of the few communities where ranching and tourism coexist in relative harmony. Cowboys wear Stetson hats to shield their sun-worn faces, skiers wear wool hats to warm frosty ears up on Mount Werner, and neither group gets in the other's way.

Settled in 1875, the Steamboat valley continued to grow as a ranching community until the early 1960s, when skiing really took hold. Today, the natives sidle up to coffee counters, discuss livestock and the weather, and in a very important way help shape the image of the ski resort. Steamboat remains a relaxed, family area, with a casual atmosphere.

Photo by Ron Dahlquist

STEAMBOAT SPRINGS, COLORADO

Steamboat gets more snow than many Colorado areas because of its location on Colorado's western slope. It's renowned for its demanding glade skiing, its size (over 1,000 acres), and its most famous resident, Billy Kidd, a two-time world ski champion, Olympic medalist, and all-around character. Billy Kidd is to Steamboat what Jerry Ford is to Vail. When not plugging his own line of ski equipment, Kidd works on the design of the ski trails and tirelessly promotes Steamboat. His style suits Steamboat—kick-ass but casual, it's a most engaging personality for a ski resort to have.

Steamboat has recently expanded and constructed more lifts (hence the lack of lift lines). Vacationers come here—it's too far from the Denver market to attract the hordes of day skiers. They know a good value, and tend to bring an attitude of fun and relaxation, an aura sadly missing at many "serious" ski areas.

THE SKIING

The skiing at Steamboat will challenge you, if only because of the ground to cover. Served by seventeen lifts—nearly as many as Vail's—including the gondola and five triple chairs, there is an uphill capacity of over 22,000 skiers per hour. So your only problem might be deciding which run to take a second or third time. During the high season (Christmas to New Year), you might have to wait in the Stagecoach gondola line. You can even avoid this jam by taking three chairs to the top—saving yourself up to forty-five minutes. Or if you're an early riser, take the gondola up to the Thunderhead Restaurant for breakfast at 8:00 or 8:30, and you'll be halfway up the mountain when the area opens at nine.

Many of Steamboat's trails are classic, western-style runs—wide-open and well groomed. There's nothing like Buddy's Run and Rainbow on Storm Peak, and High Noon and Heavenly Daze for long, wide traverses.

Try the new Three O'Clock run for bumps. And Twilight will be challenging not only for the bumps—you'll have to get through the aspen groves as well. For a thrill try negotiating the nasty moguls beneath the Priest Creed and Sundown lifts. Over on the WJW lift you'll find two wide bump runs, Drop Out and Lower Cyclone. Steamboat's glade skiing is among the finest in the West, and you'll find several runs off Storm Peak that offer steepness combined with obstacle-course demands.

If you're skiing in a group of skiers with differing abilities, you'll like the fact that lifts serve runs of varying difficulty, so you can share rides.

Meet the famous Mr. Kidd atop the slopes of Thunderheap when he's in town. At one o'clock he will lead some runs down a few intermediate trails like Heavenly Daze, with a swarm of kids in his tracks.

To get an overview of it all, a stable of hot-air balloons will take you   99

Billy Kidd, Director of Skiing, Steamboat Ski Area.

on a ride above the valley. Contact Balloon the Rockies, 879–7313, or
Balloons over Steamboat, 879–3298.

Powder Cat Tours (879–5188) conducts a very special excursion to
the Continental Divide or to the hot springs. You'll get a guided run
down the powder at the Continental Divide, and in the evening enjoy
a ranch-style dinner, followed by a snowcat ride over Steamboat's hot
springs and a soak at night under the stars.

THE TOWN/NIGHTLIFE

As Steamboat has grown, the village at the base of the mountain has
developed, too, into a full-service facility. The town has become
something of an annex. Neither, however, is really exciting. Those
wanting flashing lights and flashy blondes should consider Aspen.

Steamboat, as we said, is not the place for fast-paced nightlife,
though you might think Hersie's in Ski Time Square is a kick. Mostly
attracting a younger crowd (twenty-one and not much older), Hersie's
has loud disco, videos, no atmosphere, and a large bouncer who

checks I.D.'s and takes your $2. Faces, more popular with locals, is slightly better. And Buddy's Run in the Sheraton is a fairly ordinary hotel disco, but it can be bearable with the right crowd. An even better choice is H. B. Longbaugh's, which lets you drink $1 drafts and look out at the lower slopes. But the place to show off your windburn and the latest in ski fashion is the bar at the Ptarmigan Inn. Happy hour lasts from 11:00 A.M. until closing, and the men far outnumber the women. An established, decidedly local bar, the Tugboat is popular with ski patrol and other hard-core mountain types. Some might consider the "Boat" a dive, but we found it a very comfortable place to hang out.

In town, there's the Hatch (which is fairly seedy). Then there's the Diamond BJ Dance Hall (where you could even take your grandparents). With a huge dance floor, a country-swing band, and free dance lessons early on Tuesday nights, BJ can be the place to have some down-home fun.

You can get a light meal and great soup and sandwiches at the Mother Lodge, located both on the mountain and in town. Dos Amigos and La Montana have a battle going for position as the best Mexican restaurant on the mountain (we opt for La Montana—its frozen margaritas shouldn't be missed). Mattie Silks has fine continental fare, a long bar, and a long list of imported beers. Try Cipriani's for fine northern Italian cuisine. While it's not cheap, the pasta is homemade and delicious.

The Cover, in town, serves Cantonese cuisine for around $12. You can get excellent barbecue ribs at the Double R Bar and Bar-B-Q for under $6. Try the Pine Grove for steak. You'll dine in a converted seventy-year-old barn, but be prepared for a wait. The seafood and steak at The Brandywine are terrific, complemented by a Victorian atmosphere. One of the more established restaurants, it costs $12 to $14 per person. L'Apogee is considered by many to be the finest restaurant in town. Its classic French cuisine is prepared with an unexpected sophistication. Less imposing, and more local, the Shack has great sticky buns and coffee.

LODGING

Steamboat lacks no variety of places to stay—both on and around the mountain. Your biggest decision may be whether you want on-slope or in-town accommodations. Many prefer the ski-in/ski-out convenience of staying near the mountain, but the town has a lot more to offer in terms of local flavor and things to do.

If your choice is the mountain, try the Sheraton at Steamboat. It offers first-class hotel accommodations, with all the usual amenities. Doubles go for $80. Also on the slopes and equally expensive, the Ptarmigan Inn is a friendly, modern lodge that charges $80 for a double, $86 for three, and $92 for four.

If you're traveling in a group of four or more, however, the numerous condominiums may well prove the best deal. The Bear Claw and the Dulany are two of the more expensive choices. Four people can stay at the Bear Claw for $165 a night, while the Dulany runs $190. The condos at the Ranch at Steamboat are also luxurious, less expensive, and more secluded than most. Four can share a unit for $140. The advantage of condos is, of course, having a kitchen and the space to put extra people in the rooms if need be. For really cheap, no-frills lodging near the mountain, the Haystack Lodge is $12.25 per night and is registered with American Youth Hostels.

If you stay in town, you'll be closer to off-slope activity. The Best Western Alpiner is a typical inn, clean but without much character, while Nite's Rest Motel has waterbed and kitchen units in several of the rooms. The Best Western has doubles for $52 and six-person suites for $90. If you don't plan to spend much time in your room, the Nite's Rest is perfect. It's very inexpensive at $36 for a triple with a kitchen. For the most unusual and charming accommodations in town, try the Harbor Hotel. Many of the rooms have been individually decorated with antique English furniture. With renovations underway in 1983 and 1984, it promises to be a prime location. It's not expensive, either: a double costs $34, and four can pack in for $40.

For those who'd rather be more secluded, there are several guest ranches that take visitors in the valley. Our favorite is the Glen Eden Ranch, a half-hour from town, which has an outdoor hot tub, townhouses with kitchens, a restaurant (if you don't feel like cooking), and a free shuttle to the mountain. At $85 for a foursome, it's a bargain. And most important of all, the ranches are in the midst of the valley's outstanding beauty and serenity, where you can spot deer and elk pawing through the drifts.

ACCESSIBILITY

Steamboat is 157 miles northwest of Denver. Trailways provides bus service directly from Stapleton Airport in Denver, and Rocky Mountain Airways and AirLink Airlines fly into the Yampa Valley Airport, 22 miles away.

LISTINGS

Steamboat Ski Area
P.O. Box 771178
Steamboat Springs, CO   80477
303–879–6111

Steamboat Springs Resort Association
P.O. Box 773377
Steamboat Springs, CO   80477
303–879–0740
800–525–5502

LIFT TICKET

$21

NIGHTLIFE

Hersie's, in Ski Time Square, 879-8701.

Faces, 2305 Village Court, 879-9862.

Buddy's Run, at the Sheraton, 2200 Village Inn Court, 879-2220.

H. B. Longbaugh's, at the Sheraton, 879-2220.

The Tugboat Saloon and Eatery, 1860 Mount Werner Road, 879-9990.

Diamond BJ Dance Hall, 30080 West Highway 40, 879-7031.

The Hatch Saloon and Dance Hall, 703 Lincoln Avenue, 879-8323.

RESTAURANTS

The Mother Lode, 628 Lincoln Avenue, 879-6868; at the mountain at 1860 Mount Werner Road, 879-2839.

Dos Amigos, 1910 Mount Werner Road, 879-4270.

La Montana, 2500 Village Drive, 879-2441.

Cipriani's, 2200 Village Inn Court, 879-2220.

The Cover, 709 Lincoln Avenue, 879-7720.

Double R Bar and Bar-B-Q, 1124 Yampa, 879-7427.

Pine Grove Restaurant, 1465 Pine Grove Road, 879-1190.

L'Apogee, 810 Lincoln Avenue, 879-1919.

The Shack, 740 Lincoln Avenue, 879-9975.

The Brandywine, 57½ Eighth Street, 879-9939.

LODGING

The Sheraton at Steamboat, 2200 Village Inn Court, 879-2220.

The Haystack Lodge, 2030 Walton Creek Road, 879-0587.

Alpiner Best Western, 424 Lincoln Avenue, 879-1430 or toll-free 800-528-1234.

Nite's Rest Motel, 1601 Lincoln Avenue, 879-1212.

Harbor Hotel, 703 Lincoln Avenue, 879-1522 or toll-free 800-525-5508.

The Dulany Condominiums, 2700 Village Drive, 879-6006.

Glen Eden Ranch, 54737 Routt County Road 129, 879-3906.

Bear Claw Condominiums, 2420 Ski Trail Lane, 879-6100.

Ptarmigan Inn, 2304 Après Ski Way, 879-1730.

The Ranch at Steamboat, 1 Ranch Road, 879-3000.

TELLURIDE

If it ever got its act together, Telluride could be an awesome ski resort. Now it's pretty good, but unless major changes are made in the next decade, it will lose out to Purgatory and Crested Butte—thanks to a town divided on the "expand/don't expand" issue, remote location, lack of lodging, and a poorly designed lift system. Telluride, which offers some of the most spectacular skiing in the world plus a great town, could be in big trouble.

A former mining town, the community probably got its name from the mineral tellurium found nearby. Some folks insist, though, that the name is a shortened form of the phrase "to hell you ride." After completing your journey to Telluride, you'll most likely believe the latter explanation. Telluride is a two-hour drive from Montrose, three from Durango (if the roads are clear). Telluride is isolated, and, in fact, needs a small airport if it is to become a world-class resort. But there

Art: Bill Brown   Photo by Bill Ellizey, Telluride

TELLURIDE SKI RESORT

is deep division on the issue of expansion. If an airport were built it would bring in thousands of new skiers, and new hotels and condos would have to be built. Some fear this would ruin the haven nestled at the end of the road.

But slowly, the expansionists are winning. Plans are now underway for the construction of a lavish mountain village, a gondola, and a small airport.

THE SKIING

While experts and beginners will love skiing at Telluride, intermediates will be frustrated. Everyone, however, will be amazed by the unparalleled beauty seen from the mountain. See Forever, an exciting intermediate run from the peak, has such a breathtaking view that you may be tempted to stand there all day rather than force yourself to continue skiing.

Similarly, Spiral Stairs and the Plunge, two of the most celebrated, most demanding expert trails in the world, have you virtually skiing down into the charming little town below. Every so often you feel as though if you fall, you'll tumble right onto Main Street. It's a bit like Aspen and Vail in that respect, but a hundred times more charming.

The problem, however, is getting to all this beauty. After four lifts, fifty minutes, and a little routine skiing in between, you'll arrive at the entrance to three incredible runs and the vantage point for the spectacular view. We must say it's worth it, but you may wonder if you're on the lift in ten-degree weather with a twenty-mile-an-hour wind.

Intermediates won't be able to do much more than admire the view—the blue trails at Telluride are brief. See Forever to Pandora is the longest and it's good, but that's about it. The runs off the Palmyra lift, Polar Queen and Palmyra, are fun but rather short.

Beginners, however, after navigating their way down to the Meadows lift, will love the Prospect Meadows runs. They're wide and gentle, with just enough bump and slope to challenge, and have their own lift. But if you are a beginner, you'll regret it if you don't make the trip to the peak. Even if you can only walk down See Forever, you must see the view.

It's unfortunate that the only nonexpert route down is the Telluride Trail. (You *can* ride the Coonskin lift down, an ego crusher, but necessary at times.) The Telluride Trail, crossing Coonskin and Woozley's Way—both expert runs— is narrow, and can be dangerous, especially toward the end of the day when the trail is filled with tired beginners who have more trouble than usual navigating and avoiding the experts.

THE TOWN

How can you resist a town that has only one paved street? Casual bordering on mellow, Telluride combines historic buildings and modern surprises. Butch Cassidy robbed his first bank here, when it was a wide-open miners' town with wild saloons, painted ladies, and gunfights on Main Street. Telluride is calmer these days; now residents plan condos rather than panning for gold.

But you'll still find the same rambunctious, wild spirit in the people and businesses today. Telluride doesn't have any bars . . . it has saloons.

The Sheriden Bar, in the grand old Sheriden Hotel (in front of which William Jennings Bryan gave his famous Cross of Gold speech at the turn of the century), is the favorite hangout of locals and hotel guests. The long wood bar and ornate interior coexist peaceably with the large-screen TV showing ski films in the back. At the Last Dollar Saloon you can do some casual drinking and perhaps shoot a game of pool with a local construction worker. Some Place Else may be chastised by some for using a former altar as its bar, but we feel the gorgeous marble and carved wood piece adds a sophisticated spirit to the place. You may want to try the chili, and don't miss the steak—grill your own 12-ounce T-bone for $8.

The Roma once had the dubious distinction of being "the sleaziest bar in the world," according to one bartender. Supposedly people rode in on horseback, and fights were routine, but the Roma has long since been remodeled and gentrified, and now no one goes there.

If you're under thirty, the Fly Me to the Moon Saloon is probably the best place in town for you to go and perhaps the best at any ski resort anywhere. Featuring live music on weekends, daily specials, three pool tables, a large dance area, and the friendliest crowd in a friendly town, the "Moon" cannot be missed. It's not unusual for a bartender, in requisite Hawaiian shirt, to give you a free beer "because I feel like it"—beers are only 80 cents otherwise, and even when every other place in town is dead, the Moon is jumping.

For breakfast, locals know to go to the Flour Garden, which serves made-from-scratch pancakes and French toast, plus good omelettes. The buffet at the Sheriden is popular with skiers. This may not be saying much, but Baked in Telluride makes the finest bagels in Colorado, and is a great spot to go if you're packing a lunch.

You may have difficulty deciding where to dine. For $7 or so you can get a good burger/salad meal at the Floradora. Be warned: the chocolate fudge cake is so huge you may be too embarrassed to finish it. Silverglade, a new, somewhat high-tech spot, is earning praise for its seafood cooked over mesquite, and Sofio's is an established, well-regarded Mexican restaurant. If you want steak, go to the Powder House. The Senate used to be a place elected officials went to only in secret. This former bordello and casino (which still displays the original roulette wheel and tasteful old photos of naked women) now serves fine international cuisine to an altogether upscale crowd. The bar in the Senate has become quite the hangout for the local yuppies, too. For fine northern Italian food, try Julian's in the Sheriden. And a lovely quiet place to go for an espresso and a pastry is the Excelsior Café. But if all you want is a cheap burger and fries, go to The Underground.

LODGING

Since the shuttle bus is so convenient, there's no reason to pay lots of money for lodging in Telluride (the shuttle itself is free). And if the weather's nice, it's a short and pleasant walk to the slopes from the center of town. The New Sheriden, a classy Victorian hotel, is the town landmark and rooms rent for $30 to $50 a night. Another good deal at $30 to $55, the Dahl House is a small and homey rooming house. The Victorian Inn, the Manitou Hotel, and the Johnstone Inn are in the $40 to $60 range, while the Liberty Bell and the Oak Street Inn are cheaper still, in the $20 to $30 range.

ACCESSIBILITY

Telluride is 335 miles southwest of Denver, 125 miles northwest of Durango, and 67 miles south of Montrose. Delta, Frontier Commuter, and Trans-Colorado Airlines fly into Montrose, the closest airport, and a shuttle bus will take you from Montrose to Telluride for thirty dollars. Great Western Rent-a-Car in Montrose has a drop point in Telluride. The town operates a free shuttle that goes around town and to the Meadows and Coonskin lifts.

LISTINGS

Telluride Central Reservations
P.O. Box 1009
Telluride, CO   81435
303–728–4431 (in Colorado)
800–525–3455

Telluride Chamber of Commerce
323 West Colorado
Telluride, CO   81435
303–728–3614

LIFT TICKET

$18

BARS

The Sheriden Bar, 225 West Colorado, 728–4351.
The Last Dollar Saloon, 100 West Colorado, 728–9922.
Some Place Else, 200 West Colorado, 728–3323.
Roma, 133 East Colorado, 728–4043.
Fly Me to the Moon Saloon, 232 East Colorado, 728–3443.

RESTAURANTS

The Flour Garden, 100 South Spruce Street, 728-3502.
Baked in Telluride, 127 South Fir Street, 728-9902.
The Floradora, 103 West Colorado, 728-9937.
Silverglade, 115 West Colorado, 728-4943.
The Powder House, 226 West Colorado, 728-3622.
Sofio's, 110 East Colorado, 728-4882.
The Senate, 123 South Spruce Street, 728-3683.
Julian's, 233 West Colorado (in the Sheriden), 728-3839.
The Excelsior Café, 200 West Colorado, 728-4250.
The Underground, 121 West Colorado, 728-4790.

LODGING

The New Sheriden, 231 West Colorado, 728-4351.
The Dahl House, 122 South Oak, 728-4158.
The Victorian Inn, 401 West Pacific Avenue, 728-3684.
The Manitou Hotel, 204 South Fir Street, 728-4011.
The Johnstone Inn, 403 West Colorado, 728-3316.
The Liberty Bell, 219 West Colorado, 728-4517.
The Oak Street Inn, 134 North Oak Street, 728-3383.

VAIL

Vail is like a Disneyworld for Republicans. It's probably the kind of place your parents will love. The shops are oh-so-neat, the streets are oh-so-clean, and the food is too expensive. A pseudo-Austrian village 100 miles west of Denver, Vail has been embraced by the upper middle class as a real swank place, where maybe, if you're lucky, you'll get to see Jerry and Betty Ford.

Now, don't get us wrong: the skiing is excellent. You could ski for a full week and never get bored by the mountain, although you may tire of the town in record time—because you'll have to create your own nightly diversions in Vail.

Beaver Creek, which is an even ritzier ski area about ten miles west (the Fords and the Firestones have homes there), is developing a loyal following of its own and should be considered separately. But a real community hasn't developed around it, so we'll treat Beaver Creek as a suburban branch of Vail.

You can use your Vail lift ticket at Beaver Creek, and vice versa (we hope you're relieved to know that Vail's lift tickets are valid on the slopes of St. Moritz, Switzerland).

THE SKIING—VAIL

Vail offers ten square miles of skiing terrain, eighteen lifts, dozens and dozens of trails, and the famous deep powder of the ungroomed Back Bowls, qualifying it as the largest skiing complex in Colorado. With a perfect mix of terrain—30 percent beginner, 40 percent intermediate, 30 percent expert—no one is left out.

If you get only a week each winter to ski, Vail is ideal—it lets you start off easy and build your skills.

The Far East, Mid-Vail, Lionshead, and the Back Bowls roughly divide the mountain, and we'll highlight each.

The Far East. Flap Jack is a run the novice can enjoy, but the Far East is really expert territory. Blue Ox, Highline, and the renowned Prima and Riva Ridge will challenge the most advanced skiers. While the scenery is not outstanding, it's more wooded, reminiscent of New England. Trails on the Far East are generally less crowded.

Mid-Vail. Six lifts, the best scenery on the mountain, and a maze of trails that will keep beginners and intermediates happy make Mid-Vail's terrain the most popular. At the top of lift 3, experts will find some short but satisfying moguled runs; "bump races" are often held on Look Ma. You will find what we think is the best intermediate run in

the country, Ramshorn, at the top of crowded lift 4. Ramshorn offers large, widely spaced moguls at a pitch that is superb for intermediates, while beginners will enjoy Lion's Way and the bottom of Lodgepole.

Lionshead. This is the most popular novice area, so you'll find a lot of young children and their mothers careening about on Simba and Cub's Way. The older siblings and their fathers hit Born Free or its gentle cousin, Bwana. It's the best place to begin, but should be avoided until 11:00 A.M. or so, since it's most crowded in the morning.

The Back Bowls. For many, skiing the Back Bowls is an almost mystical experience. Experts wax ecstatic over Headwall, Morningside Ridge, and the rest in the Sun Up and Sun Down Bowls—"Heliskiing without the helicopter" is a common comment. Don't take this to mean you've been cheated if you haven't ridden lift 5. Nonexperts should stick to the Game Creek Bowl, where good intermediates can handle the black trails and novices can experience bowl-skiing on Lost Boy, or Showboat (once they've progressed). Be warned: the lift in the Game Creek Bowl develops a jam in the mid-morning, and the Bowls are great, but, ungroomed and unpredictable, they *can* be dangerous.

The sole complaint we have about skiing at Vail is the fact that it's nearly impossible to ski for very long and not see a lift or a building or some reminder of civilization.

THE SKIING—BEAVER CREEK

Beaver Creek is sedate and sophisticated. Perhaps the aura of multi-million dollar homes creates a quieter atmosphere. It also benefits from following on the heels of twenty-five years of ski resort development. Beaver Creek is a sort of miniature Vail. Designed with the intermediate in mind, only the most advanced skier won't enjoy it.

Intermediates: avoid the crowd at the main lift, #6, and start instead on #12 across the road (this lift carries you right over President Ford's backyard). You may like the wide and fairly steep glade runs that begin at the peak, or you can cut over to the newly developed Larkspur Bowl. Red Tail, the best intermediate run, is parallel to three double-diamond trails. Experts appreciate them because they're served by their own lift (#9). And you beginners will want to head straight for the top, where a number of trails provide fine glade skiing.

NIGHTLIFE—BEAVER CREEK

Hah.

Jerry Ford may have been a decent president, but he and his buddies weren't exactly known for getting down. After skiing Beaver Creek, people hit their Jacuzzis, eat an elegant dinner, review their investment portfolios for a while, and go to bed.

The lounges at the luxurious lodges, McCoy's and Drinkwater Park, both in the Village Mall, are about the only two bars around. Not too exciting, though they do attract their share of ski-patrol rowdies on occasion.

If you want nightlife you'll have to go to Vail.

NIGHTLIFE—VAIL

The town of Vail is divided roughly into two sections, Lionshead and Vail Village, which are connected by a free, efficient shuttle bus system.

Vail's discos are rather revolting. You know that feeling of pity you get when you see a middle-aged couple doing the Hustle. You'll find yourself feeling that a lot in Vail; especially at Rumors and Shadows, the two most popular discos.

Rumors disco, in the Westin Hotel, is what you'd expect to find in a luxury hotel—small, contrived, and expensive. Shadows, larger and more popular, has lots of chrome and blinking lights, and caters to an older crowd.

You may want to try the Sundance Saloon, which has developed a strong local following. It's got a large bar and a lovely view of the mountain. The bar at Cyrano's is classy, but by far the most popular spot for a drink after skiing is Trail's End at the Gondola.

Popular doesn't necessarily mean best. Our vote goes to The Slope, a totally relaxing place where patrons sit on the floor, lean against cushioned backrests, and watch great ski flicks and W. C. Fields shorts. Though the bartender sometimes has to wake someone on the floor at closing time, The Slope often gets rowdy. After all, when everyone's lying on the floor and getting plowed, certain thoughts tend to predominate.

Both Lionshead and Vail Village have many fine restaurants—but few are cheap. And while excellent dining is easy to find, you are almost always guaranteed a wait. Where to find good but moderately priced food? It's limited, but not impossible to obtain.

For breakfast, try the Pancake House in the Village Inn. The fare is standard IHOP, and you should be full for under $5. Frasier's in the Gondola Building has a limited breakfast menu and the Clock Tower Cafe in the clock tower on Bridge Street does interesting things with eggs.

Huge burgers and great soups make Blu's Beanery in Vail Village a real find. It's good for lunch and dinner, but more expensive at night.

When it's time for dinner, the Pancake House still offers the cheapest menu (except for McDonald's) if you want burgers and fries. Fans of Chinese food rave about the Hong Kong Café in Vail Village—especially its lemon chicken—and it will cost you $11 or so. For a great brunch and a diverse though expensive dinner, try Cyrano's, also in Vail Village. You'll get a kick out of their classy Art Deco atmosphere.

But you don't have to go far to find Vail's most exciting restaurant—exactly 39 feet, 7½ inches north of the Gondola rests Bart and Yeti's. Named for two dogs (Bart fathered Jerry Ford's pooch Liberty, and he has offspring in both Robert Redford's and Henry Kissinger's homes), this casual place is probably the last of Vail's old "regular" restaurants serving good burgers, ribs, and "samiches." We recommend you spend an evening here.

"Cheap food, warm beer, poor service"—the motto of Ruby's, located a few miles west of Vail in Eagle-Vail, is one-third right: the food is cheap, and it's good. The burgers and ribs are great, but the real treat at Ruby's is the lack of tourists. Make the effort to get there.

LODGING—VAIL

Vail is made up of lodges, shops, and restaurants, with the emphasis on lodges, and you won't find many budget choices. Go with at least four people if you want a price break. The cheapest rates are available in early December, January, and April. "Value packages" (seven nights of lodging and five days of lift tickets, or four nights' lodging and three days' lift tickets) will save you as well.

The Lionsquare Lodge, the Plaza Lodge, the Golden Peak House Lodge, Antlers, and the stately, old-faithful Lodge at Vail are all within walking distance of the lifts, and offer every conceivable amenity. A one-bedroom apartment per night is cheapest at the Plaza ($115 or so), moderate at the Lionsquare, Golden Peak, and Antlers ($160 or so), and most expensive at the Lodge at Vail ($230).

There *are* some comparatively inexpensive places to stay, with the emphasis on comparatively. Vail 21 and the Vail Village Inn are in the $50 to $100 range during off-peak times and are convenient to the lifts. The Sandstone Creek Club, across the interstate, gets $50 to $80 for its rooms, and the Inn at West Vail, a Best Western, charges $45 and up. If you want a good deal, and don't mind some rowdies, you can't beat the Roost. A bedroom and bath for one is a steal at $30 (off-peak), and a studio with a kitchenette costs $80.

LODGING—BEAVER CREEK

If you thought accommodations at Vail were expensive, then cast your gaze at Beaver Creek. The Centennial, the Charter, Creekside, Kiva, and the Poste Montane are the main lodges, and suffice it to say that the cheapest one bedroom/one bathroom at the Charter costs $125 a night during low season.

ACCESSIBILITY

Vail is 100 miles west of Denver, right off Interstate 70. Rocky Mountain Airways flies into Avon, 10 miles west of Vail. Shuttle service is available from the airport. Trailways provides service from downtown Denver and Stapleton Airport, and there are a couple of charter van services from Stapleton, too. The town operates a free shuttle bus within Vail, and buses from Vail to Beaver Creek cost $1.

LISTINGS

Vail Resort Association
241 East Meadow Drive
Vail, CO   81657
Information: 303–476–1000
Central Reservations: 800–525–3875

Beaver Creek Central Reservations
P.O. Box 7
Vail, CO   81658
303–949–5750
800–525–9132

LIFT TICKET

$21

BARS

McCoy's, Village Hall at Beaver Creek, 949–7158.

Drinkwater Park, Village Hall at Beaver Creek, 949–5001.

Rumors, in the Westin Hotel, 1000 South Frontage, 476–7111.

Shadows, in the Marriot Mark Resort, 715 West Lionshead Circle, 476–4444.

The Sundance Saloon, in the Sunbird Lodge, Lionshead, 476–3453.

Trail's End, in the Gondola Building, 476–6121.

The Slope, below Baxter's at the top of Bridge Street, 476–5296.

RESTAURANTS

Pancake House, in the Village Inn, 100 East Meadow Drive, 476–2207.

Frasier's, in the Gondola Building, 476–3488.

The Clock Tower Café, 232 Bridge Street, 476–5306.

Blu's Beanery, under Krismar at Vail Village, 476–3113.

Hong Kong Café, Wall Street, Vail Village, 476–1818.

Cyrano's, at the top of Bridge Street, Vail Village, 476–5551.

Bart and Yeti's, 39 feet and 7½ inches north of the Gondola, 476–2754.

Ruby's, in the Eagle-Vail Business Center, 949–5212.

LODGING—VAIL

Lion Square Lodge, 660 West Lionshead Place, 476–2281.

The Plaza Lodge, 291 Bridge Street, 476–4550.

Golden Peak House Lodge, 278 Hanson Ranch Road, 476–5667.

Antlers, 680 West Lionshead Place, 476–2471.

The Lodge at Vail, 174 East Gore Creek Drive, 476–5011.

Vail 21, 610 West Lionshead Circle, 476–1350.

Vail Village Inn, 68 South Frontage Road East, 476–5622.

The Sandstone Creek Club, 1020 Vail View Drive, 476–4405.

Best Western Inn at West Vail, 2211 North Frontage Road West, 476–3980.

The Roost, 1783 North Frontage Road West, 476–5451.

LODGING—BEAVER CREEK

The Centennial, 845–7600.

The Charter, 949–6660.

Creekside, 949–7071.

The Kiva, 949–5474.

Poste Montane, 949–6400.

WINTER PARK

A Lone Star State visitor gave a pretty solid analysis when he said, "If Vail's your Mercedes and Aspen your Porsche Targa, then Steamboat is a Ford half-ton and Winter Park is a Chevy station wagon." Not exactly literary, but not bad for a Texan.

Winter Park isn't fancy, flashy, or outrageously expensive. It is, however, a practical vacation spot attracting dedicated fans year after year who come to enjoy tranquility and low prices.

You'll find yourself riding the lifts with a lot of skiers from Denver. It's not surprising. Denver skiers know their own turf. They know where to go close by for good and inexpensive skiing. Adult tickets cost $18 for a full day during regular season. Children thirteen and under and seniors sixty-two to seventy ski for just $7 a day, and if you're over seventy, you ski for free.

Winter Park has come a long way since it opened in 1940 with one rope tow. Since then it has expanded to an 800-acre skiing complex. There is 80 percent more skiable terrain now since Mary Jane on Winter Park's eastern flank was developed. It's now possible to ski two distinct sides of the mountain—the old area which is mostly intermediate, wide open runs, and the "Jane" side, with its predominantly expert trails.

Winter Park emphasizes skiing, not nightlife. The town itself is just starting to grow and in the future there will be hotel complexes and condos, but if you desire hot nightlife you'll go home disappointed. Except for a few in Old Town Winter Park, most restaurants and accommodations are two miles down U.S. 40. A vacation in Winter Park will be more serene than sizzling, but you are guaranteed an easygoing western atmosphere.

THE SKIING

Don't pay attention to the fact that Winter Park has "only" 800 acres of skiable terrain. (For comparison of some nearby areas, Breckenridge has 1,150 and Steamboat 1,100). It's one of the best run areas anywhere, with enough variety to keep you from noticing that the resort isn't physically as large as many others. Except for the chair over to Mary Jane, lines rarely exceed ten minutes on the lifts.

Your first decision of the day will be whether to begin on Mary Jane or Winter Park, a decision which will depend largely on skiing ability. Though there is one short beginner run at the base, Mary Jane is for the advanced skier. Trails at the Jane are tough and moguled. A   115 twelve-minute ride up the Iron Horse drops you within reach of a short patch of tree skiing on Pine Cliffs or Sluicebox, or several shorter black diamond runs such as Arrowhead Loop or Golden Spike. Move over to the Challenger chairlift and you'll find not only a shorter lift line, but longer and harder runs, such as Derailer, Rail Bender, and Phantom Bridge. There's also Little Ten, and for an easier ride, Sleeper. You won't get bored at Mary Jane.

You can get to the more toned-down Winter Park from the Jane via Olympia Spur and the Iron Horse chairlift. Though both Allan Phipps and March Hare are great beginner slopes, don't feel alarmed when you end up in a little pocket that requires a chairlift-ride rescue—the Looking Glass area has a way of sneaking up on you. But then take a five-minute ride on the Looking Glass chair, and it's an easy run to the midmountain Snoasis restaurant. The Olympia chair will get you out of Looking Glass as well, but don't take it unless it's a warm day—the ride takes fifteen minutes.

Expert slopes on the Winter Park side are good but short. Balch is rarely crowded, and little Pierre gives a tough, short ride. But most notable of all is Outhouse, bordering the two sides of Winter Park. From Sunspot (at the top of the new triple Zephyr lift) an imposing sign warns that only those with skis 185 centimeters or more in length can ski this long, beautiful, and knee-grinding run. The 185-centimeter rule is a thoughtful consideration for expert skiers, as the moguls tend toward a nice uniform shape, without those nerve-racking cliffs off the downslope side.

THE TOWN/NIGHTLIFE

Restaurant happy hours make up the bulk of the nightlife in Winter Park. The Mary Jane Lounge at the Slope in Old Town Winter Park features a DJ and live music. At the newer Stampede in Cooper Creek Square, you can enjoy disco or country and western.

Granby is down U.S. 40 about forty miles, and don't forget Denver is just seventy miles away. In other words, you don't *have* to stay in Winter Park if your spirit dictates a wild evening.

RESTAURANTS

Off to an early start? Try the Coffee and Tea Market in the Balcony House right in Winter Park ski area. You won't want to pass up their coffee and fresh pastries. Competing with freshly baked breads daily and a small but delicious breakfast menu is the Carver Brothers' Bakery, which also serves good submarine sandwiches.

If you're up for bratwurst and sauerkraut, try the Gasthaus Eichler Restaurant. Dinner prices are $12 or so. For Mexican food—and a few oriental dishes—Lani's Place, next to the Husy Station in Fraser, is a must. And Lani's won't empty your pocket. For carry-out Chinese food, the Wok Inn on U.S. 40 in town is a good stop and fairly inexpensive.

For a complete steak dinner, you have a choice between the Shed, in Winter Park, and the Longbranch, in Granby; both run about $10. L. C. Benedict's varied menu includes prime rib, trout and shrimp scampi, and, of course, eggs Benedict. The atmosphere is Victorian, and dinners are about $12, lunches around $5.

For superb dining, Expectations at the Slope in Old Town Winter Park vies with Cooper's Restaurant for first place and top dollar. Expectations features veal, lamb, and seafood, while Cooper's concentrates on northern Italian cuisine along with a few Rocky Mountain favorites such as trout and steak. Enjoy, but expect to pay $18 for dinner at either.

One local favorite is Deno's Swiss House and Coachman Tavern. Burgers, chicken-to-go, barbecue, and Mexican food in a publike, friendly setting. All this, and satellite TV, too, for around $8.

LODGING

Lodging in Winter Park consists primarily of ski lodges and condominiums. Many of the lodges offer the Modified American Plan (MAP), providing breakfast and dinner for a fixed rate. Since this arrangement can be convenient and economical, the trick is to find a lodge that serves good food and is close to the slopes. The Timber House Ski Lodge, with ski-in access to the lodge from Winter Park, offers a variety of rooms, some much nicer than others, and hearty meals served at long wooden tables. Guests return yearly to Timber House to enjoy the outdoor hot tub, sauna, and the fireplace in the living room. Brenner's Ski Chalet, slightly smaller though similar to Timber House, is just through the woods. Not as old, Brenner's also has private access to the Billy Woods trail for ski-in convenience at the day's end. We have a list of their assorted rates at the end of this chapter.

The Viking Lodge in town is very basic, not exceedingly personable, but without the Modified American Plan requirement. Doubles run $35 to $60.

The Best Western High Country Inn is close to the skiing, and has a friendly atmosphere. Meals are optional, and from 4:00 to 6:00, $4 will buy you all the drinks and hors d'oeuvres you want. Doubles are $63, including meals.

John Martling's Morning Star Ranch is far from the glittering crowd. It's quiet and small—eight rooms—and convenient to cross-country trails. Singles and doubles cost $50 per person, including lift tickets.

Winter Park has a youth hostel in town. Dorm-style rooms are in trailers, and the hostel is within walking distance of all town conveniences. Cost is $9.

Of the numerous condominiums and condominium management

companies, one of the more noteworthy is the Iron Horse Condominiums, located on the mountain near Mary Jane. Beaver Village, a lodge on U.S. 40, also has several condos nestled in the woods in a very serene setting. In Fraser, only a drive away, are the Twin Rivers Condominiums, with several different units available. Their Sun Song units are well appointed and, typical of Winter Park lodging, relatively isolated and quiet.

ACCESSIBILITY

Winter Park is only seventy miles from Denver on good roads. Continental Trailways buses serve the town.

LISTINGS

Winter Park Recreational Association
Box 36B
Winter Park, CO   80482
303–726–5587
800–525–3304

Winter Park Chamber of Commerce
78846 Highway 40
Winter Park, CO   80482
303–726–8334

LIFT TICKET

$18

RESTAURANTS

Coffee and Tea Market, at the base ski lodge, 726–5095.
Carver Brothers' Bakery, 93 Grand County Road 7, 726–8202.
Gasthaus Eichler, Park Place, 726–5133.
Lani's Place, 213 Zerex, Fraser, 726–9674.
Wok Inn, 78916 Highway 40, Fraser, 725–9583.
The Shed, 78672 Highway 40, 726–9912.
The Longbranch, 185 East Agate, Granby, 887–2209.
L.C. Benedict, 78336 Highway 40, 726–8104.
Expectations, 1161 Winter Park Drive, 726–5727.
Cooper's, 78930 Highway 40, 726–8059.
Deno's Swiss House and Coachman Tavern, 78911 Highway 40, 726–5332.

LODGING

Timber House Ski Lodge, Box 32, 726–5477. Room and board in a
six-person dorm, $32 a day; singles, $46; three to four per room, $36

a day. All rates include breakfast and dinner. Five- , six- , and seven-day packages available.

Brenner's Ski Chalet, 115 Grand County Road 716, 726–5416. Three nights' lodging and two lift tickets, singles $128 to $182. Seven-day packages with seven nights' lodging and six days' lift tickets, $309 to $429 singles; three per room, $309 to $396.

The Viking Lodge, Box 89, 726–5324, or toll-free 800–421–0130. Also eight-person cabins with kitchenettes, $120 a day.

Best Western High Country Inn, U.S. Highway 40, 726–5566 or toll-free 800–528–1234.

Morning Star Ranch, 933 Grand County Road 8, 726–8118.

Winter Park Hostel, Box 3323, 726–5356.

Beaver Village Ski Chalet, 79303 U.S. Highway 40, 726–5741, or toll-free 800–525–3561. Singles range from $60 to $69. Rates include breakfast and dinner.

Condominiums: Prices vary according to season. Generally one bedroom costs about $100, two bedrooms about $150, three bedrooms about $200.

Utah

Utah's ski resorts have stood in the shadow of Colorado's mountains for years. Western skiing meant Vail or Aspen, not Snowbird or Park City. Mention Utah, and Mormons and deserts came to mind, not powder and moguls. But the tales kept filtering back from those adventurers who did ski Utah—tales of challenging mountains with chest-high powder, inexpensive lift tickets and no lift lines. By the 1970s, skiing Utah had a cachet of its own. The chic ski set from New York's Upper East Side started to drop the name of Snowbird rather than Snowmass, and people were impressed.

Despite Utah's growing popularity, a number of myths about skiing in the state still survive, so we'll try to kill them off here, once and for all:

You can't drink in Utah.

False. Utah does have archaic liquor laws, but you can drink by joining a "club." Membership is $5 for two weeks, and you can bring friends. Beer is also available in many nonclub settings, and liquor stores are fully stocked. So drinking is no problem.

Utah is a flat desert.

False again. Utah has incredible snow: 500 inches a year at the higher resorts. The snow is so dry that it never turns to ice. Actually, Utah has the best snow in the country.

Most of Utah's ski areas are located around Salt Lake City. You can ski them all inexpensively by staying at a cheap motel in town and driving to the mountain each day. Snowbird, Alta, Park City, and several other areas are a forty-five-minute shuttle bus ride away.

Each major area has a distinct personality. Park City, for instance, is a major "destination" resort. It has all the amenities: restaurants, bars, hotels. You can find better snow elsewhere, but Park City is polished. Up the road is a ski area designed for the very rich—Deer Valley. And Alta and Snowbird rest atop a different canyon. Because they're higher up they get better snow. Alta has been around forever. The skiing is incredible, and lift tickets at Alta cost just $10. Lodges

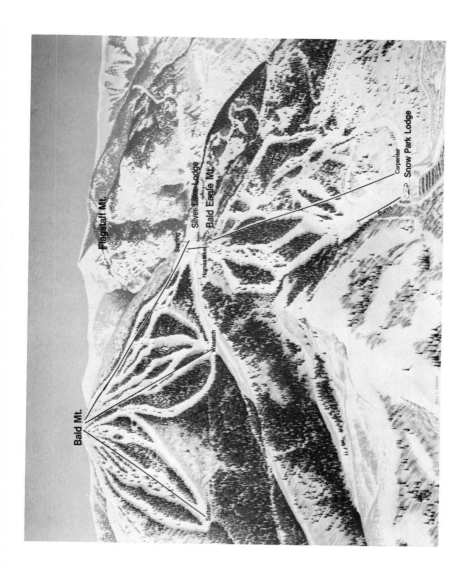

Flagstaff Mt.

Silver Lake Lodge

Bald Eagle Mt.

Sterling

Homestake

Wasatch

Bald Mt.

Sultan

Burns

Carpenter

Snow Park Lodge

that provide breakfast and dinner are the only housing. Snowbird, just a half-mile down the road, provides elegant, expert skiing. Condos and hotels provide the housing. There are some bars and restaurants, but the superb skiing is the draw. The only thing to say against Alta and Snowbird is that nightlife is negligible.

ALTA

If Clint Eastwood skied, he would probably ski Alta. This resort offers a taciturn crowd, tough slopes, low prices, and no-nonsense service; Clint would feel at home. A man named Chuck Morton has ruled Alta for more than a quarter of a century, and little has changed under his reign.

Skiing costs $10 a day, and guests still stay in lovely trailside lodges where breakfast and dinner are served. One of the few things that have changed, and for the better, is the addition of the Albion chairs, which add substantial beginner and intermediate terrain. Any skier will enjoy Alta.

Like its neighbor Snowbird, Alta comes up short on nightlife. Set at the end of a road, with no "ski village," it is truly isolated. But Alta is a sociable place, and you'll meet your fellow guests at breakfast and dinner. It draws the sort of people who like a sense of adventure, of skiing the way it was twenty years ago before the sport was discovered.

THE SKIING

Alta has thirty-five trails, with seventeen rated expert, fourteen intermediate, and four beginner. There are two chairs reserved for novices, Albion and Sunnyside. The two longest chairs, Collins and Wildcat, serve mostly expert trails. Germania is by far the most popular chair, and caters to the intermediate and expert runs. Mambo, another favorite, is an intermediate run. Intermediates can also cruise Devil's Elbow and Roller Coaster on the Sugarloaf chair. Expect to do some traversing, though; Alta has a flat midsection that can lead to long treks.

Diving down most of the mountain, Alf's High Rustler is the classic run at Alta. You'll have to traverse from the Germania trail and walk up a little hill to reach it; the top is very steep. The Supreme chair has some fun intermediate and expert trails and never draws the line that Germania does. The Sidewinder run, off to the east, can have some of the best trail conditions since it gets so little use.

But with the great powder available, people love to go off the trails. The most common route is to traverse over from Germania onto Mount Baldy, but whole sections of the mountain have been left untrailed. Eagle's Nest and Greeley, both beyond Alf's High Rustler, are 122 two wonderful wooded sections that drop off into a great bowl.

NIGHTLIFE

Don't be surprised when you go to the bars and see little children—
Alta does have a family atmosphere.

You can go to Snowbird for excitement, but you won't find much
there either. The sole restaurant (outside of the lodges) is Shallow
Shaft, a good steakhouse.

LODGING

As mentioned, all lodging is on the mountain, except for a few nearby
condominiums.

The Snowpine Lodge has a dormitory setup where you share a
quad room, and is Alta's greatest bargain. As is the case with all of
Alta's lodges, breakfasts and surprisingly good dinners and maid service are included. A three-day package, including lift tickets, meals,
and room, costs just $129, five days go for $215, and a week costs
$291.

Goldminer's Daughter is a solid step up from Snowpine but still
pretty basic. Rooms come with private baths, televisions, and phones.
The dorms, however, don't have a TV. The dorm bedroom, with four
twin beds (as opposed to Snowpine's bunks) costs $43 a night, with
dinner and breakfast. A bedroom with one bed for two people costs
$50, and a large bedroom which holds four costs $45 apiece. Goldminer's has hot tubs and saunas.

The Alta Peruvian, a pleasant lodge, draws a young crowd. Prices,
which include breakfast, lunch, dinner, and lift tickets, start at $55 for
a dorm. Rooms with just a wash basin (no bath) start at $62 a person
per night, while a suite with one or two bedrooms, a large sitting
room, and fireplace (all this houses four people) costs $82 per per-
son. The Peruvian also has an outdoor pool.

The Rustler, one of the newer establishments, starts at $52 for a
dormitory room, a price that includes only breakfast and dinner, not
lift tickets. The Rustler is an elegant, lovely facility. A room with no
bath costs $60. A large room with a bed, a sofa bed, and a balcony
costs $95 per person. The Rustler has saunas, a heated pool, and
Jacuzzis. And the Rustler bar seems to have the most excitement
(which isn't saying much).

The Alta Lodge, the most distinguished and traditional, has dorm
rooms at $58.50, which includes breakfast and dinner. Small, shower-
less rooms cost $63.50, and a combination bedroom-sitting room
starts at $84. Rooms in the new addition are larger, and many include
a fireplace and bath, and also cost $84. The Alta Lodge has two
indoor pools and a sauna. With its superb cuisine and dignified
charm, the Alta Lodge draws the loyalists who have been coming to
Alta since before the first chairlifts were even installed.

There are also two nearby condominium complexes that are discussed in the Snowbird chapter.

ACCESSIBILITY

Same as Snowbird (see chapter).

LISTINGS

Alta Ski Resort
Alta, UT   84092
801–742–3333

LIFT TICKET

$10

RESTAURANTS

Shallow Shaft, 742–9906.

LODGING

Snowpine Lodge, 742–3274.
Alta Peruvian, 742–3000 or toll-free 800–453–8488.
Rustler Lodge, 742–2200.
Alta Lodge, 742–3500.
Goldminer's Daughter, 742–2300 or toll-free 800–453–4573.

DEER VALLEY

Deer Valley is making the same wager as Beaver Creek: that there are a lot of middle-aged, intermediate skiers out there who aren't too concerned about budget options. For instance, waiters refill your coffee cup in the *cafeteria;* there are no ski racks—skiers check their skis at a guarded corral; a reservation system limits the number of skiers. Of course, luxury has a price.

Deer Valley is under development by the redoubtable Stein Eriksen (father of Sugarbush in the East) and when completed will be one of the most elegant resorts around. It's one man creating his own dream.

In the summer of 1984, the resort underwent a large expansion: over two hundred new condo units and two new triple chairlifts increased the skiing terrain by almost 30 percent.

Right now, Deer Valley is too new to really be judged; how well it will work remains to be seen. Skiers at other areas say everything from "Eriksen is making millions" to "It's going bankrupt." Though neither opinion is accurate, there is a lot of confusion about the area, and many regard Deer Valley as a novelty to be tried once.

THE SKIING

Five "padded" triple chairs and one double chair serve thirty-two trails on a mountain that is mainly intermediate. It has a 2,200-foot vertical drop, which comes from two separate mountains, one atop the other. Deer Valley, in terms of size and challenge, is not in the same league as Alta, Snowbird, or Park City, but then, it doesn't want to be.

Deer Valley is just a mile up the road from Park City, so nightlife and additional restaurants are just a short shuttle-bus ride away.

The Stein Eriksen Lodge offers elegant accommodations and elegant dining. Seven nights and six days of skiing cost $925 per person, four-person occupancy. The Deer Valley resort costs $601 for the same package during the regular season.

LISTINGS

Deer Valley Resort Company
P.O. Box 1525
Park City, UT   84060
801–649–1000
Lodging: 800–453–3833

LIFT TICKET

$25

PARK CITY

Park City is trying to compete with the big guys and is doing a sensational job of it. Of all the Utah ski areas, only Park City can be called a complete "destination" resort, with enough hotel rooms, restaurants, and, above all, nightlife to host large crowds. In times past, advanced skiers faulted Park for lacking expert terrain, but with the construction of Jupiter chair, the resort will challenge any skier.

It has, despite its development, retained an incredibly friendly and enthusiastic crowd. The staff bubbles with goodwill, and the skiers seem to enjoy themselves here more than anywhere else. Park has avoided the "macho" mentality that some of its neighbors have developed, and it remains charmingly unpretentious.

Perhaps it's the little touches that make the resort and its trails the most polished we've seen—signs placed on trails where the lifts pass overhead, and restaurants on the trails which serve good food. The Mid-Mountain Lodge, for example, has Swiss cuisine at affordable prices.

Park is a huge mountain, with enough terrain to keep any skier busy. Eleven chairs and a long gondola serve sixty-nine trails plus several bowls. The mountain has distinct areas for beginners, intermediates, and experts.

Salt Lake residents still look down at Park for several reasons. Lift tickets run more ($22) at Park than at any local resort except Deer Valley. Park isn't as challenging as Snowbird or Alta, and doesn't get as much snow. Its base is a couple of thousand feet lower than Alta's or Snowbird's, and "only" gets 350 inches of the world's best snow. As an out-of-stater, these points may not concern you: lift tickets are only a fraction of a skier's budget, and much more goes on at Park at night. If you're an expert and tire of Park, you can always take the daily bus run to Snowbird and Alta.

THE SKIING

Park has "Western America's longest gondola," but it's usually *not* the way to ski the mountain. During peak season it gets twenty-minute lines, and doesn't really take you to the best skiing. The Ski Team chairlift, however, will let you ski to King Consolidated, which has ten wide intermediate trails, or to Prospector and Lost Prospector, which have some good, more advanced bump runs. These are three of Park's most popular chairlifts. You can get to some neighboring expert and intermediate trails on the Motherlode chair, but the lift for advanced trail skiing is Thaynes, which serves some excellent expert bump runs. Thaynes never gets lines and has runs like The Hoist, which, in theory, is limited to skiers on 190-centimeter skis and longer—this rule actually does make for bigger moguls.

Experts take the Jupiter Bowl chair for bowl and chute skiing. Set on the highest part of the mountain—10,000 feet—the snow here is significantly better. With steep skiing, the easiest way down is probably the West Face. Because the trees on the right side of the lift catch snow and then slowly let it drop, it's always like skiing fresh powder. Many also hike over to Puma Bowl and McConkey's Bowl—twenty strenuous minutes—to some great, untouched powder. The two bowls lead into Park's trail system.

During the day, if Park can't deliver enough powder skiing, the helicopters can. Utah Powderbird Guides charge between $175 and $245 for seven runs, depending upon the areas skied. They occasionally offer half-days starting at $80.

Located at the local golf course, White Pine Touring Center has just five kilometers of tracks. As well as renting skis, they offer half-day and full-day tours. Skiing up the snowmobile tracks in the adjoining Thayne's Canyon is the closest route around. You can also buy maps and get advice on local back-country routes.

The Ski Utah Interconnect, which lets you ski all five local areas in one day, is discussed in the Snowbird chapter.

THE TOWN/NIGHTLIFE

For after-dinner action, Park City has Utah's best nightlife—a series of elegant bars, plus beer and dance halls. All the major bars are located on Main Street. Of them, the best are Janeaux's, the Black Pearl and the Cowboy Bar, and the latter two have dancing. As mentioned previously, in Utah you must join a club before you can drink hard liquor. Membership costs $5 for two weeks' admission, and your card also admits five of your friends. Of course, all the clubs are glad to have you join.

RESTAURANTS

Haute cuisine in Utah refers more to the altitude. Park has a lot of good restaurants, but you're probably better off passing up the expensive ones, with one exception. The Glitretind Gourmet Room in Stein Eriksen's Lodge, a mile up the road, serves elegant, delicious dishes at high prices. On the more conventional side, Mileti's Italian restaurant is also very popular, and the Eating Establishment, which adds a creative flair to all its dishes, is probably Park City's best value. Scrooge's has an eclectic menu in the $8 to $10 range. Barbecue, and pretty good barbecue at that, is served at Texas Red's Pit Barbecue. Baja Cantina and Utah Coal and Lumber offer good Mexican food. Both are reasonable, but Utah Coal is especially so. You can get good steaks at the Grub Stake. Janeaux's, Adolph's and Car 19, all in the $10 to $18 price range for entrees, are Park City's more refined restaurants. Car 19 added some of Park City's former gondola cars to their decor.

Park City is home to Robert Redford's United States Film and Video Festival. Redford owns the nearby Sundance ski resort and sponsors this festival of independent filmmakers. The annual event takes place in January. In February, Park hosts the United States Ski Team Celebrity Classic, where you get to watch the stars ski.

If the trails didn't tire you out, the Prospector Athletic Club, with its racquetball courts, swimming pool, and weights, will. Tennis enthusiasts can play at the Park Meadows Racquet Club, which has Park's only indoor tennis court.

LODGING

A cornucopia of pseudo-Victorian houses remains from Park's boom of the 1970s, leaving the village looking like a fantasy vision of a mining town. Park's lodging has great variety, all within walking distance or a short bus ride of the mountain.

For all but budget lodging, call Park's toll-free reservation numbers, 800–453–2849 and 800–453–5789. The accommodating people there will arrange anything from a hotel room to a house, and they can help with buses from the airport and such, too.

On the budget side, Acorn Chalet Lodging, a friendly, simple establishment fifty yards from the slopes, has hotel rooms starting at $35, and a two-bedroom condo at just $80. The Chateau Apres Lodge, just 150 yards from the slopes, holds 132 people. The chateau, whose motto is "Stay in nonluxurious luxury," is a steal. You can put two people in a room for $35, or four can stay for just $45. Dorm space is $10 a person, and meals are also inexpensive—$5.75 for a complete dinner. Retaining the old mining boom-town atmosphere at a less expensive price are the Star Hotel and the Alpine Prospector. Carol runs the Star Hotel, which offers a private room, breakfast, and dinner for $32.50 a night. Food is served family-style, and devoted customers tack their business cards on the wall. It's a ten-minute walk to the slopes. The Alpine Prospector, right nearby, charges only $44 for a quad and $26 a night for a single. Baths are shared. Other bargains include The Digs, a three-bedroom Victorian home with "early Salvation Army" decor that goes for $120 a night for up to ten people, and The Ore House, a three-bedroom chalet on the parking lot that costs $80 for four people.

Five minutes away from the lifts, the Prospector Square Hotel has studio lofts for just $85 a night. If you plan to stay just a night or two, many hotels won't be too accommodating, but Holiday Inn's The Yarrow doesn't mind. Singles start at $72 a night.

Park has a covey of condominiums on the slopes; it's best to let the reservation service direct you. Some of the nicest include the Snow Flower, Silver King and Silver Cliff Village. Sweetwater has had problems in the past, but is now under new management. Snow Flower, the least expensive of the first three, will cost $105 for a studio, $195 for two bedrooms, and $300 for four bedrooms and a loft, per night, on a "regular" week.

ACCESSIBILITY

Everyone flies to Salt Lake City, and Park City Taxi and Lewis Brothers Stages run vans to the airport. The ski resort is just forty-five minutes from the airport on fairly easy roads. Rental cars are easily available (Hertz even has an agency in town), but aren't really needed.

LISTINGS

Park City Ski Area
Box 39–SD3
Park City, UT   84060
801–649–8111

Park City Reservations
P.O. Box 1330
Park City, UT   84060
800–222–7275

LIFT TICKET

$22

BARS

The Black Pearl, 350 Main Street, 649-6793.
The Cowboy Bar, 268 Main Street, 649-4146.

RESTAURANTS

Adolph's, 1541 Thayne's Canyon Drive, 649-7177.
Baja Cantina, at the base of the resort, 649-2252.
Car 19, 438 Main Street, 649-9338.
Eating Establishment, 317 Main Street, 649-8284.
Grub Steak, Prospector Square, 649-8060.
Janeaux's, 306 Main Street, 649-6800.
Mileti's, 412 Main Street, 649-8211.
Scrooge's, 502 Main Street, 649-9627.
Glitretind Gourmet Room, Stein Eriksen Lodge, 649-3700.
Texas Red, 440 Main Street, 649-6993.
Utah Coal and Lumber, 201 Heber Avenue, 649-9930.

LODGING

Acorn Chalets, 1314 Empire Avenue, 649-9313.
The Digs, P.O. Box 75, 649-8221.
The Ore Haus, c/o 3915 Pluto Way, 277-7296.
Silver Cliff Village, P.O. Box 1360, 649-8200.
Snow Flower, P.O. Box 957, 649-6400.
Silver King, P.O. Box 2818, 649-5500.
Chateau Apres Lodge, 1299 Norfolk Avenue, 649-9372.
Claimjumper Hotel, 573 Main Street, 649-8051.
Prospector Square Hotel, P.O. Box 1698, 649-7100.
Holiday Inn The Yarrow, 1800 Park, 649-7000 or toll-free 800-225-5785.
Alpine Prospector's Lodge, 151 Main Street, 649-3483.
Star Hotel, 227 Main, 649-8333.

MISCELLANEOUS

Utah Powderbird Guides, P.O. Box 57, Snowbird, 649-9739.
Ski Utah Interconnect, 307 West 200 South, Suite 5005, Salt Lake City, 534-1779.
White Pine Touring Center, P.O. Box 417, Park City, 649-8701. (It's the golf course nearest the mountain, off State Highway 224.)
Prospector Athletic Club, Prospector Square 649-6670.
Park Meadows Racquet Club, 1200 Little Kate Road, 649-8080.

SNOWBIRD

"Slow down," reads the notice on a chalkboard at Snowbird, "and give the beginners a chance." The message sums up Snowbird—it's an advanced skier's mountain. Beginners deserve some sympathy at Snowbird, not because they're always getting run down by the experts, but because they're missing out on perhaps the best advanced and expert terrain in the country: mogul fields spread over steep slopes; "bottomless" powder in bowls and chutes; a long, European-style tram.

Not only does Snowbird offer ample off-trail skiing in Utah's fabulous powder, but it has (conservatively counted) sixteen expert slopes; the longest stretches the entire 2,900 vertical feet of the mountain. There is, however, a short chairlift and adequate terrain for beginners. It's the intermediate who will really feel left out. Snowbird counts twelve of its thirty-two trails as "intermediate," but when they have names like Cat Track or Easiest Route, you know they're hurt-

ing. An intermediate could ski Snowbird for a weekend; a longer trip would be better spent at Alta or Park City.

You may find the lack of signs at Snowbird annoying, so bring a map if you want to know what trail you're on.

Another drawback is the nightlife. Your local library has more action than Snowbird. Located next to Alta at the end of a long, twisting road, both resorts rely on day skiers, not vacationers. Neither Snowbird nor Alta has large resort villages. Snowbird enthusiasts say the skiing is so superb and challenging that everyone is too tired to play at night.

Snowbird's boasts about its snow aren't idle. An annual accumulation of 500 inches of powder (measured at the *middle* of the mountain) keeps Snowbird open 212 days a year. Spring skiing is superb, with more than 200 inches of snow in March and April. Snowbird also provides a very useful ski host/hostess program. The guides have a rendezvous point at 10:00 and 1:00, at which times they'll give a personalized tour of the mountain. This is for anyone, from the intermediate who wants to try the tram to experts searching for the best powder.

All the lodges at the base are owned by Snowbird, and are luxurious but sterile condominiums and hotel rooms. The same can be said for the restaurants, which are well designed but not particularly exciting.

THE SKIING

Snowbird's aerial tram holds 125 and ascends the 2,900-foot vertical in eight minutes. There are seven double chairlifts as well. You'll have to wait twenty minutes or more for the tram on peak weekends of Christmas, and there are rarely lines on the chairs. The tram takes you to the long expert runs, and classics like Regulator Johnson. As well as serving intermediate and beginner terrain, the two Gad chairs also take you to the chairs that lead to more difficult areas, such as Gad 2 and Little Cloud.

The off-trail ski opportunities at Snowbird are ample. Near the Black Forest there is some easy tree skiing, while the truly daring can hike up near the top of West Twin Peak. It's strongly recommended that you consult a ski patrol member before you ski the unbelievably narrow chute amid the rocks. The Peruvian Cirque is very steep; for a thrill, ski patrol members go straight down when the area is closed.

Of the more traditional trails, those off Gad 2 offer some of the steeper bump runs around. If the snow gets hard-packed, Silver Fox and Dalton's Draw usually retain the best conditions. Intermediates can ride down the tram and take Chip's Run (it's the one marked Easiest Way Down). Otherwise, they're limited to the chairs, with most of their trails on the Gad 2 lift. Big, wide, and easy, Big Emma was named after the first madam in the old mining camp. For beginners, the Chickadee lift runs in the opposite direction of the other chairs and is on the other side of the parking area.

Even though it's an hour's drive from Park City to Snowbird, you can actually ski both in the same day—without using your car. Five of the major ski areas (Park City, Brighton, Solitude, Alta, and Snowbird) have combined to form the Ski Utah Interconnect Adventure. Accompanied by a guide (and all on downhill skis), you'll do some hiking (at altitudes up to 11,000 feet) and some skiing in the woods, but you'll be able to ski all five areas in a single day. Skiing three resorts (Solitude, Brighton, and Alta) costs $30 a person and lasts five to six hours; four resorts (Snowbird, Alta, Brighton, and Solitude) costs $45 and also lasts five to six hours; skiing all five (starting at Park and ending at Snowbird) costs $60 and lasts eight hours. The trips start at the first resort mentioned and end at the last.

Helicopter skiing is discussed in the Park City chapter.

RESTAURANTS AND NIGHTLIFE

The only dancing you'll find is at the Tram Room Bar; the other two bars, the Eagle's Nest and the Lodge Club, are quiet lounges.

Snowbird's excellent restaurants don't make up for a nonexistent nightlife. You can get a good steak at the Steak Pit, while for more elegant, continental dining you might try the Golden Cliff and the Lodge Club. The food at the Mexican Keyhole is good, and surprisingly reasonable, and the Forklift is right near the tram. The Birdfeeder is dreary. The only other options nearby are the restaurants at Alta's lodges.

LODGING

As mentioned earlier, with the exception of two nearby condominium complexes all the lodges at Snowbird are owned by the resort. Thus, the Cliff, the Lodge at Snowbird, the Turramurra and the Iron Blosam all cost the same price. As a rule of thumb, the newer the building, the better the quality. During the regular season, a bedroom will cost $76 a night, studios start at $81, and a studio with an adjoining bedroom costs $180 for two people; add $7 for each additional person. The rooms are fairly small, with fold-down beds, sofa beds, and the like. All the condominium complexes are generously equipped with saunas, pools, etc.

The Hellgate Condominiums are located halfway between Alta and Snowbird. Most suites have balconies and a separate sitting room. A two-bedroom condo costs $190 a night; three bedrooms cost $240, and four bedrooms (up to eleven people) cost $290.00. You can ski between the Blackjack Condominiums and Snowbird. Studios cost $80, one bedroom costs $135, two cost $185, and three bedrooms cost $235.

The atmosphere at Snowbird is nondescript; the new and concrete buildings make you feel like you're in a very nice set of corporate headquarters. If you want more ambiance, stay at Alta.

ACCESSIBILITY

Snowbird is about forty-five minutes by bus from the airport. Salt Lake City is served by nearly all the major airlines, by Greyhound and Trailways bus lines, and by Amtrak.

LISTINGS

Snowbird Ski Resort
Snowbird, UT   84092
Information: 801-742-2222
Reservations: 801-532-1700, or toll-free 800-453-3000.

LIFT TICKET

$15 ($19 with tram pass)

BARS

The Tram Room, 521-5040.
The Eagle's Nest, 742-2222.
The Lodge Club, 742-2222.

RESTAURANTS

The Steak Pit, 521-6040.
The Golden Cliff, 742-2222.
The Lodge Club, 742-2222.
The Mexican Keyhole, 742-2222.
The Forklift, 521-6040.

LODGING

All Snowbird lodges are handled through central reservations.
Hellgate Condominiums, 742-2020.
Blackjack Condominium Lodge, 742-3200.

California

One of the Sierra Club's first losses was in a battle to try to prevent the commercialization of Lake Tahoe. It lost, and so, we're sorry to say, did the resorts.

But despite the encroachment of gambling and the fast-food industry, it remains beautiful. The panorama from the ski areas is incredible, and where else can you ski and windsurf in the same day? As long as you're on the mountain it's heavenly—descend into South Lake Tahoe and you're in a neon nightmare.

Now, about the mountains: Squaw is gigantic and well planned, rivaling Vail or Aspen. While smaller, Alpine Meadows has something Squaw lacks: personality. Forty minutes down the road from Squaw and Alpine Meadows, Heavenly Valley shows the results of mixing casinos and skiing.

Down the road you'll find some resorts that thrive on their isolation. Sugar Bowl, reachable only by gondola, is becoming popular with families, while Kirkwood, with more challenging slopes, provides one of the best "retreat" vacations in the country.

Tahoe itself used to be hard to reach, and the area still mainly draws a West Coast crowd. However, the growth of the Reno and South Lake Tahoe airports have made it readily accessible to the entire country.

Tahoe is home to several festivals. Snowfest, an annual nine-day celebration in nearby Truckee, begins the first Saturday in March. It includes ski races, taco-eating contests, street dancing, and, of course, lots of beer. Winterskol is held the first week of February each year in Incline Village (another Tahoe resort); national and celebrity ski races highlight the week.

For those who like to indulge in a little of everything, Alpine, Squaw, Heavenly Valley, and Kirkwood offer five- and six-day interchangeable lift passes, a great way to see and ski all four areas.

California's other large ski centers—Mammoth and June mountains—sit several hundred miles away. Mammoth, the larger of the two, has a real West Coast style while June, quieter and smaller, offers a more slow paced alternative.

ALPINE MEADOWS

Alpine Meadows seems to have the sense of youth, fun, and vitality that its neighbors have lost. Though it used to be considered a small adjunct to Squaw, Alpine has become recognized for its own merits. Though admittedly not as massive as Squaw, its trails offer a fine selection, especially for the intermediate. It's a marvelous place to be in spring—with the southern exposure, lakefront locale, and huge deck.

Just five minutes by car from Tahoe City, Alpine straddles Ward and Scott peaks, and includes the long ridge between them. Since both sides of that ridge have lift service, you can ski down any face of the mountain: north, south, east, or west. The resort's main lodge and several chairlifts are less than five years old. No lodging is available on the mountain itself; however, there is a free ski shuttle to and from the lodges on the nearby shore.

Alpine draws a young crowd—ski bums, college students, and weekend moonlighters. The atmosphere is exuberant, and you'll find people gathered on the deck when the sun peeks out, or in the social hall in the main lodge, which easily entertains 1,500. Having fun comes naturally at Alpine.

THE SKIING

Alpine has every kind of skiing—the top pokes out above the timberline, the middle is edged with glades, and the bottom is laced with well-designed slopes. Snowfall averages over 400 inches a year. One of the nicest features of Alpine Meadows is the "sun bowls" on the southern exposure where the sun warms the air, yet the snow usually stays cold, making these wide-open mogul fields good for springlike skiing even in the middle of winter.

If you're a beginner, you should stay on the bottom parts of the mountain because the summit is steep. Intermediates can follow the sun all day, skiing east to west across the various exposures of the mountain.

But it's advanced skiers who are in luck here, able to choose between the snow bowls (Wolverine, Alpine, and Sherwood) and the lower glades under the Yellow and Roundhouse chairs. The truly adventurous can attempt the remote and less skied Beaver Bowl or the short Palisades/Upper Saddle region on Ward Peak, which has steep, deep-powder terrain.

138   To ski the expert trails you must get to the tops of Ward and Scott

peaks. There are two chairlifts to the 8,637-foot peak of Ward, and one chair and T-bar climb to the summit of Scott. Ranking near the toughest in the Tahoe region are the Scott Chute and Promised Land runs on Scott. The ridge between the two peaks contains miles of intermediate runs that lead down into grooved, high-altitude basins.

If the snow starts to melt, head up toward the summit and ski Wolverine and Alpine Bowls. Sherwood, on the south, can occasionally get soft and bare.

Lift lines are a problem only on weekends, when the wait can be up to twenty minutes, with shorter waits on the higher lifts. But after the first ride, you can ski the rest of the day without seeing the bottom.

THE TOWN/NIGHTLIFE

Tahoe in the winter isn't all snow and frigid air. It's windsurfing, scuba diving, hang gliding, and snowmobiling. There is a ski triathlon held each winter which includes sailing on Lake Tahoe, running to the mountains, and skiing. For dual-sports enthusiasts, a ski-sail package is available—do both on the same day. For more traditional winter activities, there is sledding and nordic skiing. And, for a more sedentary sport, gambling is just an hour away.

At night, many of the folks from Alpine and Squaw head to Tahoe City. The big night spot is Gatsby's, a big pub with nightly entertainment and dancing. For a friendly atmosphere and a well-stocked bar, try Honkers. Dinner and drinks are pleasant at Rosie's Cafe. If you want to rub shoulders with the jet set elite, go to Caesar's Tahoe Club Lookout in Stateline, an elegant dancing spot. Be sure to get dressed up first.

In Tahoe, you can eat anywhere from a local diner to a head-spinning casino. Next to Alpine, the River Ranch, a fairly fancy restaurant, charges $8 to $18 for dinner. Tahoe City's Tahoe House has elegant Swiss cuisine, and runs $10 to $17. For a fancy yet inexpensive dinner that will cost you between $6 and $13, try Honkers Bar and Grill. Their menu ranges from pasta to beef and fish. An excellent chain from the East, The Chart House, has great steaks and seafood, plus a nice bar. Dinner runs from $7 to $15. Less expensive and more outlandish, duck blintzes can be had at Rosie's Cafe. For Mexican cuisine in the $4 to $8 range there's the Hacienda del Lago. The Marina Creperie is a good place for breakfast and lunch specials.

If you'd like to nurse a few beers and have some pizza (it's rather expensive), head out to Carnelian Bay to Mountain Mike's Pizza. South of Tahoe City, the Grubstake Café is an inexpensive and nice place for dinner.

LODGING

Alpine has a strong selection of low-priced lodgings. The Family Tree Restaurant and Motel has comfortable rooms and an inexpensive restaurant. Singles cost $36, with each person $2 extra. The Tahoe Vintage Inn has lovely rooms. For $40, you and whomever else you can squeeze in get bed and breakfast. The Franciscan Lakeside Lodge charges $40 for a room with a kitchen, and $65 to add on a living room. Just north of Alpine, the Seven Pines Motel costs $30 per room. In the same area the Fire Lite Lodge charges $25 for a single, $28 for a double.

The Alpine Motor Inn, very close to both resorts, offers breakfast and kitchen units. It costs $45 for doubles, $40 for singles. The Lake Pines Motel runs $40 with a kitchen, $25 without. On the upscale side, the Tahoe Marina Lodge has beautifully furnished bedrooms with lakefront views. One bedroom costs $70, two go for $95, with discounts for longer stays. If you like heights, stay at the Pepper Tree Inn, a high-rise tower with a view of the lake. It costs $40 on weekends. The Charmey Chalets, closer to Nevada, offers spacious garden patio units and saunas. Rooms average $50 to $70.

ACCESSIBILITY

The most convenient route to Heavenly, Alpine, and Squaw is to fly directly into South Lake Tahoe airport, serviced by Pacific Coast Airways, AirCal, Aspen Airways, and Golden West, and take the bus or rent a car. The major airlines fly into Reno International, about fifty miles away. From Reno, you can take a bus for $8 each way or rent a car. The roads to the ski areas are all major routes, well maintained in the winter.

LISTINGS

Alpine Meadows Ski Corporation
P.O. Box AM
Tahoe City, CA   95730
916–583–4232
Central reservations: 916–583–1045

LIFT TICKET

$22

RESTAURANTS AND BARS

Tahoe House, 625 West Lake Boulevard, 583–1377.
Honkers Bar and Grill, 640 North Lake Boulevard, 583–5700.
River Ranch, Highway 89 and AM Road, 583–4264.
The Chart House, Roundhouse Mall, 583–0233.
Gatsby's, 850 North Lake Boulevard, 583–5131.
Hacienda del Lago, The Boatworks, 583–0358.
Rosie's Cafe, 571 North Lake Boulevard, 583–8504.

Mountain Mike's Pizza, Carnelian Bay, 546-2537.
Marina Creperie, 760 North Lake Boulevard, 583-0051.
Grubstake Café, 5335 West Lake Boulevard, 525-5505.

LODGING

Family Tree Motel, 551 North Lake Boulevard, 583-0287.
Tahoe Vintage Inn, 4170 Ferguson Avenue, 583-6091.
Franciscan Lakeside Lodge, 6944 North Lake Boulevard, 546-7234.
Seven Pines Motel, 279 Bear, Kings Beach, 546-9886.
Fire Lite Lodge, 7035 North Lake Boulevard, 546-3036.
Alpine Motor Lodge, Alpine Meadows, 583-4266.
Lake Pines Motel, 2815 Lake Forest Road, 583-3209.
Lake of the Sky Motor Inn, 955 North Lake Boulevard, 583-3305.
Pepper Tree Inn, 645 North Lake Boulevard, 583-3711.
Charmey Chalets, 6549 North Lake Boulevard, 546-2529.

HEAVENLY VALLEY

The majestic mountain of Heavenly Valley rises to 10,167 feet above Lake Tahoe—almost high enough to overcome tacky South Lake Tahoe below. Almost.

Heavenly Valley calls itself America's largest ski resort, and spanning a high mountain ridge on the border of California and Nevada, it *is* huge. The slopes allow you to ski two states in one day. But Heavenly Valley is caught in a dilemma—is it a ski resort or an annex to a casino? Most skiers who come to Heavenly Valley have gambling in mind.

So if you don't want to lose time getting to the gambling, Heavenly is the place to go. South Lake Tahoe and Stateline, two very touristy, very crowded, and very commercial towns, are within walking distance. And the casinos never close. The classiest are Harrah's and Caesar's; you've missed something if you leave without dancing at Caesar's or taking in a show.

For another kind of thrill, Heavenly offers the only helicopter skiing in the Sierras. It costs only $40 to $50 a day for a guide, lunch, and 10,000 feet of vertical.

THE SKIING

Heavenly is an overrated mountain. On the California side, the lower slopes are so overskied there can be mush and even bare patches. Large crowds produce long lines. The upper slopes are less crowded, but only two of them are rated tougher than intermediate. Also, many trails merge halfway down the California side, producing traffic jams. The bottom slopes in California are legitimate expert trails, but nowhere near as good as Squaw's. Intermediates tend to flood them. At the top, Ellie's is a fine expert trail.

While fewer people ski the Nevada side, because it is more remote, it has more runs and better conditions. You can reach these trails via the Dipper, Stagecoach, and Galaxy chairs. You'll find the Galaxy and Bonanza bowls are particularly good runs. It takes seven miles to reach the bottom of the Galaxy trail.

Though clearly not enamored of Heavenly, we must admit its good points. Despite a summit of over 10,000 feet, Heavenly is heavily forested with trails that tend to wind through the woods, like in New England. The views—Lake Tahoe from the California side and the desert from the Nevada side—are stunning.

THE TOWN/NIGHTLIFE

The only thing at the base of Heavenly is a large lodge, cafeteria, and bar. The real action takes place minutes away in the casinos and clubs of South Lake Tahoe and Stateline. It's like a video parlor for adults—everyone dashes off from one neon fantasy to another. But it costs more than a few quarters.

South Lake Tahoe is reminiscent of the boardwalk at Atlantic City. Since all the casinos are within a few blocks of each other, you can wander back and forth. Caesar's and Harrah's are the classiest and most expensive. The High Sierra, Barney's, and John's Tahoe Nugget are better bargains and a bit more funky. Although obviously designed for the big spender, the casinos can also be enjoyable for college students and amateurs. You should take advantage of the special deals that Caesar's, Harvey's, the High Sierra, and the Tahoe Nugget offer. Just by making an appearance you can get free drinks and inexpensive brunches.

If you tire of the casinos, drive twenty minutes into Nevada to After Dark, a nice getaway for dancing and drinking. Or, right in South Lake Tahoe, the Dory's Oar is a wonderfully romantic rendezvous.

To mingle with the locals, try the Mine Shaft or the First Draft Choice. They specialize in cheap beer and plenty of talk.

RESTAURANTS

Not surprisingly, the food is better at the casinos. Two of the best are the Summit at Harrah's and the Sage Room Steak House. Outside the casinos, Carlos Murphy's combines Mexican and Irish Cuisine. Cabbage and beef tacos? Sounds strange, but they're great. The Bitter Creek Saloon and Café is a superb place to drink and eat a light meal. Western food is its specialty, and dinners average $6 for a meal and a drink.

Cantina Los Tres Hombres has a strange menu, but serves good Mexican food for around $6. For good seafood or steaks, try the Chart House in nearby Stateline. The Brother's Place, off the main drag, is a favorite of the college crowd. If you're looking for good, inexpensive American food, try the Crystal Cafe. Waterwheel South has a large menu of Mandarin and Szechuan cooking, with a $4 to $10 range. There are also myriad diners and fast-food joints.

LODGING

Again, the casinos, especially Caesar's and Harrah's, are the nicest places to stay. They're all about a mile from Heavenly via free shuttle buses. You'd be smart to get a package plan unless, for example, you want to spend $150 for a night at Harvey's. Caesar's includes four days' skiing and four nights' lodging, double occupancy, for $239 per person. At Harrah's the same package is $267. The Sahara Tahoe and Harvey's (good food and great nightlife) each charge between $180 and $200 for the same deal. There are other deals—a seven-night/six-day package is $396 at Caesar's and $445 at Harrah's.

Another choice is condominiums. Right on the water, Lakeland Village is beautiful. Concept Sierra Sitzmark Condominiums and Summit Condominiums, both at the base of the mountain, are within walking distance of the slopes. Heavenly North Condominiums are at Heavenly Valley North (the Nevada side) and they aren't inexpensive: a package where four can share a two-bedroom unit with four nights' lodging and four days' skiing runs $199 to $226 per person during nonholiday periods. Three-bedroom condominiums are also available.

South Lake Tahoe has loads of inexpensive, mom-and-pop hotels, but you'll have to do some searching to avoid those that are more rundown.

El Nido Motel, quiet and comfortable, is a bargain at $28. The Timber Cove Lodge has extensive lakefront facilities and costs $57 on a weekend. Your basic, simple motel, Brooke's is $36 on weekends. One block from the casinos, the Holiday Lodge runs $70 on a weekend, and the Tahoe Driftwood Lodge charges $44 for nice but small rooms. For a quiet location on the golf course, there's the Tahoe West Motor Lodge, which comes with breakfast at only $48. The 7–11 Motel has a marvelous location; close to Heavenly and casinos, it's a bargain at $35. Finally, if you've come to Heavenly to ski and fool around, take advantage of Fantasy Inn. With three locations to serve you they include all the prerequisites—hot tubs, mirrors, waterbeds, house champagne . . . adult movies . . .

ACCESSIBILITY

The Lake Tahoe Airport is just ten minutes from Heavenly and is served by AirCal. Most major airlines fly into the Reno airport, fifty-five miles away, and there's regular bus service between the Reno airport and South Lake Tahoe. Greyhound offers frequent bus service, and there are free shuttles running all over the place. To drive, it's three and a half hours from San Francisco, and an hour and a half from Reno.

LISTINGS

Heavenly Valley
P.O. Box AT
South Lake Tahoe, CA   95705
916–541–1330

Heavenly Central Reservations
P.O. Box 2180
Stateline, NV   89449
702–588–4584
800–822–5922 (in California)
800–824–5150 (outside California)

LIFT TICKET

$24 (credit card); $23 (cash)

NIGHTLIFE

After Dark, Roundhill Mall, Zephyr Cove, 588–4113.
The Midnight Mine, Zephry Cove, 588–5608.
The Dory's Oar, 1041 Fremont Avenue, South Lake Tahoe, 541–6603.
Cuckoo's Nest Cafe, 2452 Highway 50, South Lake Tahoe, 541–0873.
Caesar's Tahoe Club Lookout, Stateline, 588–3516.
The Mine Shaft, 807 Emerald Bay Road, South Lake Tahoe, 544–0456.

RESTAURANTS

Carlos Murphy's, 3678 Lake Tahoe Boulevard, South Lake Tahoe, 542–1741.
Cantina Los Tres Hombres, Highway 89 and Tenth, South Lake Tahoe, 544–1233.
The Chart House, Kingsbury Grade, Kingsbury, 588–6276.
The Summit, Harrah's, Stateline, 588–6611.
The Sage Room, Harvey's, Stateline, 588–2411.
Crystal Cafe, Highway 50 at Ski Run Marina, South Lake Tahoe, 544–2429.

Waterwheel South, Crescent V Shopping Mall, Highway 50, South Lake Tahoe, 544-4158.

Bitter Creek Saloon and Cafe, 3350 Sandy Way, South Lake Tahoe, 541-9460.

The Brother's Place, 888 Emerald Bay Road, South Lake Tahoe, 541-7017.

LODGING

Barney's Casino, Stateline, 588-2455.

Caesar's Tahoe, Stateline, 588-3515 or toll-free 800-648-3353.

Harrah's Lake Tahoe, Stateline, 588-6611 or toll-free 800-648-3773.

Harvey's, Stateline, 588-2411.

John's Tahoe Nugget, Stateline, 588-6288.

Sahara Tahoe, Stateline, 588-6211.

El Nido Motel, 2215 Highway 50, South Lake Tahoe, 541-2711.

Fantasy Inn I, 3677 Lake Tahoe Boulevard, South Lake Tahoe, 541-6666.

Fantasy Inn II, 924 Park Avenue, South Lake Tahoe, 544-6767.

Fantasy Inn III, 790 North Lake Boulevard, Tahoe City, 583-8578.

Timber Cover Lodge, 3411 Highway 50, South Lake Tahoe, 541-6722.

Brooke's Lodge, 3892 Lake Tahoe Boulevard, South Lake Tahoe, 544-3642.

Holiday Lodge, 4097 Laurel Avenue, South Lake Tahoe, 544-4101.

Tahoe West Motor Lodge, 4082 Pine Boulevard, South Lake Tahoe, 544-6455.

7-11 Motel, 3640 Lake Tahoe Boulevard, South Lake Tahoe, 541-7400.

Tahoe Driftwood Lodge, Laurel Avenue and Poplar, South Lake Tahoe, 541-7400.

JUNE MOUNTAIN

June Mountain is a small, friendly, and less crowded alternative to Mammoth Mountain, fifteen miles south. Compared to that of its enormous neighbor, June's skiing isn't nearly as challenging or diverse, its snow isn't as deep, and its nightlife is almost nonexistent. But June is a fine mountain for an intermediate who wants to escape Mammoth's crowds for a few days, and for a beginner who prefers to learn in a less hectic environment.

Our chapter on June will be relatively brief, because the mountain and town itself are quite small. The resort offers only six lifts and about twenty trails, and the town has about two dozen lodges and just a handful of restaurants. June is proud of its image as a sleepy, relaxed village—"the Switzerland of California," according to the brochures—and no one is too keen on changing the quiet grace of the area.

THE SKIING

Though June has only six lifts to serve its split-level mountain, lift lines are rarely a problem—except, sometimes, at the end of the day. You see, June's toughest trails are on the bottom half of the mountain, known as the Face. Since they are indeed steep, a problem arises each afternoon: how do beginners get home? Most sacrifice their egos and ride the #1 chair down the mountain, while the more daring decide to risk tumbling down the one intermediate trail to the base.

The Grand Chalet Schweizerhof, the main building on the mountain, is halfway up, as is the departure point for most of the skiing. The intermediate runs like Sunrise and Lottie Johl are fun, but they often have long flat runoffs. The expert trails on the top can be handled by most adventurous intermediates. Every skier should take the #3 chair to the top, however, because the views from the summit are stupendous.

THE TOWN/NIGHTLIFE

The tiny town of June Lake has a permanent population of less than 500, but most everyone is involved with serving skiers. There are plenty of lodging possibilities from which to choose, but for real restaurant and nightlife options, most people prefer to travel down the road to the Mammoth area.

Two restaurants in the village offer a rather diverse selection. The Carson Peak Inn is probably the best restaurant in the area and offers a broad menu and "California rustic" atmosphere. The Normandy Inn is a good deal more plush, and it's a very cozy choice for a quiet drink in the late afternoon. Most of the lodges and motels have small restaurants and bars, too.

LODGING

The June Mountain area is a much cheaper place to stay than Mammoth. The Haven, Lake Front Cabins, June Lake Pines, and Silver Pines Chalet all have apartments or cottages in the $25 to $60 range. The Silver Pines also offers dorm space for $15 a night, as does the Fern Creek Lodge. The June Lake Villager and the June Lake Motel are decent, standard motels with prices from $35 to $55 or so.

ACCESSIBILITY

June Mountain is fifteen miles north of Mammoth Mountain on Highway 395. For further information on getting to the area, see the Mammoth Mountain chapter.

LISTINGS

June Mountain
P.O. Box 146
June Lake, CA 93529
619–648–7733
Reservation Service: 619–648–7844 or toll-free 800–462–5589

LIFT TICKET

$20

RESTAURANTS AND BARS

The Carson Peak Inn, Route 158, 648–7575.
The Normandy Inn, Route 158, 648–7998

LODGING

The Haven, Knoll Avenue, 648–7524.
Lake Front Cabins, Knoll Avenue, 648–7527.
June Lake Pines, Route 158, 648–7522.
Silver Pines Chalet, Gull Lake Road, 648–7469.
Fern Creek Lodge, Route 158, 648–7722.
June Lake Villager, Route 158, 648–7529.
June Lake Motel, Route 158, 648–7547.

KIRKWOOD

Many ski resorts sacrifice excellence and intimacy for size and volume. If you've been searching for a ski retreat that combines quality and warmth, seek no more.

Thirty miles south of the commercial South Lake Tahoe district, Kirkwood borders on the fabulous Mokulomnee Wilderness region. Lovely and quiet, the village is entirely self-sufficient—it even has its own power generator. To add to the solitary nature, the nearest major town is an hour away over two mountain passes.

Facing east and south along a ridge made up of four peaks, Kirkwood can hold its own against anything in the Lake Tahoe region. While not as big as Squaw, Kirkwood offers trails with a good variety and better snow than at Tahoe. And, just as important, lift lines are nonexistent except on one base chair.

With an attentive and hospitable staff, friendly and accessible skiers, it's not surprising that Kirkwood attracts so many families and couples.

The benefits are debatable, but Kirkwood plans to expand by 75 percent over the next ten years, turning the village into a ski town and introducing some badly needed nightlife.

THE SKIING

Kirkwood is very wide, with a 1.5-mile ridge along the top. From this ridge to the midway point lie the truly challenging expert trails, particularly on lifts #3 and #5. Glove Rock and Thimble Peak at the summit, both well above the timberline, offer beautiful cornice runs, as well as slopes with wide playgrounds of deep powder. The lower three-fourths of the mountain is gladed with nicely sculptured trails.

Because of Kirkwood's width, the skiers of all classes can separate. The lower, more gentle slopes and the Kirkwood chair, where the terrain is almost flat, are for beginners. Intermediates can have an easy day skiing under lifts #1, #2, and #7. Just remember to take the right trail when you come down for lunch or you'll end up a mile from where you intended to be.

THE TOWN/NIGHTLIFE

There are only four places to drink, eat, and dance. There isn't even decent television reception. The Kirkwood Inn is a rustic, thick wooden inn from the old pioneering days, decorated with hats and old skis. For $3 to $5 you can eat chicken, burgers, chili, and the like. This inn has no lodging, though. On the northern end of the slopes, Snowshoe Thompson's Bar and Restaurant is open all day. It serves great pizza, pasta, subs, salads, etc., plus beer for $3.50 a pitcher. The Whiskey Run Restaurant and Bar is in the nondescript eight-story condominium tower. It serves basic food at basic prices—$5 for lunch, $10 for dinner. The Whiskey Run is a main hangout, with its game room, pool table, and tunes. For a touch of class there's the Snowflake, with European and American cuisine at $10 to $15. People stay till the bar closes at 10:00 P.M.—along with most of Kirkwood.

LODGING

Although many people choose to stay in nearby Meyers or South Lake Tahoe—which means a drive to the mountain each day—Kirkwood is designed for people who stay there.

The condominiums (the sole on-mountain lodging) are within easy walking distance of the lifts. Rooms are elegant, but due to the previously mentioned poor reception, they don't have televisions. Studios cost $65, one bedroom goes for $85 to $125, two-bedroom units cost $110 to $165, and three bedrooms cost $175.

Sorenson's, about twelve miles from Kirkwood, is an all-season resort for backpacking, fishing, and ski touring. Cabins start at $35 a night. It also has a home-style restaurant, good for breakfast.

Caple's Lake Resort, just outside the village, is its own self-sufficient community, with restaurant, lounge, and general store. Cabins and guestrooms run from $30 to $48 a night, or $220 for the week. It's comfortable, has a superb view, and offers a good ski package with Kirkwood.

Kay's Silver Lake Resort, ten miles away, has fully equipped housekeeping cabins, a store, and a gas station. Rent starts at $30 a night.

ACCESSIBILITY

Many people fly to Lake Tahoe or drive from the coast. Lake Tahoe is thirty miles away. Highway 88 (a two-lane road) is the only road into Kirkwood, and although the California Department of Transportation works hard to keep it open, the road sometimes closes. Chains or four-wheel drive are required. No trains or buses stop at Kirkwood. For road conditions, call the California Department of Transportation, 916–577–3550.

LISTINGS

Kirkwood Ski Resort
P.O. Box 16
Kirkwood, CA 95646

General: 209-258-6000
Lodging information: 209-258-7247
Snow report: 209-258-3000

LIFT TICKET

$20

RESTAURANTS

The Snowflake, 258-7225.
Snowshoe Thompson's, 258-7315.
Whiskey Run Restaurant, 258-8101.
Kirkwood Inn, 258-7304.

LODGING

Reservations for condominiums can be made through Kirkwood.
Sorenson's, Hope Valley, 916-694-2203.
Caple's Lake Resort, P.O. Box 8, 258-8888.
Kay's Silver Lake Resort, 48400 Kay's Road, Pioneer, 258-8598.

MAMMOTH MOUNTAIN

Welcome to skiing, Los Angeles-style. Mammoth Mountain, with twenty-three chairs, two gondolas, two T-bars, and a Poma, rivals the southern California freeway system in complexity. And with over a million skiers a year, it draws almost as large a crowd.

Mammoth attracts the stereotypical southern California crowd. Christie Brinkley clones flash their smiles and gold chains, while handsome males strip down to parade their bare chests and bulging biceps. Mammoth's ski season lingers into late June and sometimes even July, and the beautiful young Californians take full advantage of it. Nevertheless, it's wonderful for the older crowd—skiers over sixty-five ski free.

Mammoth is an excellent mountain for skiers of any ability. The upper half is well above the timberline, providing much open space and many bowls. There is a ridge that stretches out for over a mile, allowing expert skiers to pick and choose from numerous bowls, chutes, and faces. The bottom half is perfect for intermediates and novices, with enough trails to keep them busy for a week.

Even though Mammoth is a solid seven-hour drive from Los Angeles and six from San Francisco, it draws large crowds on almost any day of the week. One-hour waits on the gondolas are common on weekends. But if you like crowds, the town of Mammoth Lakes can be a lot of fun at night.

THE SKIING

Writing a complete trail description of Mammoth could fill this whole book. Dave McCoy ran a rope tow up the mountain on Thanksgiving weekend in 1941, and Mammoth opened. Even then, people flocked—there were over 250 skiers on the slope. Ever since, McCoy has been building and building.

1982 saw the addition of two new triple chairs that opened up significant expert terrain. Chair #23, anchored to the rocks between the Drop Out and Wipe Out chutes, provides easy access to a large amount of terrain that used to require a long traverse. Chair #22 is the first up Lincoln Mountain and opens up many advanced ski slopes.

Dave's Run (after McCoy) is a favorite of fine skiers. You ski the traverse along the ridge from the gondola top to a wide-open face with a pitch of almost 50 degrees at the top. Another expert route, Felip's, is a narrow rock chute that twists to the right halfway down. Aptly named are: the Paranoid Chutes, Drop Out, Wipe Out, Climax, the Cornice, the Huevos Grandes. Good tree skiers can find un-tracked bowls and chutes all over the place. Local favorites include the trees off the ridge on chair #12, as well as the trees by chairs #4, #16, and #10.

On the lower half of the mountain, trails wind among the pine and fir trees. Although crowded on weekends, chairs #3 and #5 are very popular. Each leads up its own little mountain, with many selections of runs and snow conditions. Chair #19 offers access to several great bowls and some good intermediate tree-skiing, and it's rarely crowded, even on weekends.

For the view alone, a trip to chair #14 is worthwhile. On the back side of Mammoth's ridge, the chair provides access to anything from bumps to bowls to trees. Advanced skiers can take a fifty-foot hike and drop over the ridge into the Paranoid Chutes or Scottie's Run.

Even first-time skiers have their choice of lifts and runs. Chairs #6, #7, and #11 offer wide-open slopes. More experienced beginners will take lifts #1, 2, 4, 8, and 10 through 21 (excluding 14). Intermedi-ate skiers also make use of these chairs, but the terrain is such that the runs are skiable by anyone who can make a good snowplow.

Mammoth likes to say that its snow is better than the common "Si-erra cement." It has a point. The snow on the eastern side of the Sierras does tend to be drier than at Tahoe. Mammoth is also famous for its corn-snow skiing in the spring. Warm, sunny California days followed by cool, clear nights combine to "corn up" the snow. Spring skiers like to move up the mountain as the day becomes warmer. By afternoon, you might want to head down to fish for your supper in one of the nearby lakes and streams.

TOWN/NIGHTLIFE

With over thirty-five restaurants and bars, you will be able to find whatever—or whoever—you want. The nightspots range from re-laxed conversation spots and hot dance clubs to cowboy joints. But remember, the town is several miles away from the resort.

The places to dance in town are Whisky Creek and the Rafters. While you will find other spots that offer live entertainment and danc-ing, these places are "where it's at." Their bands are excellent, drinks are good, there's enough room to dance and partners to choose from. The Village Inn is a cowboy bar with live music and a big dance floor. You may even be able to sit in on a hand or two of poker.

You can watch ski videos on the big-screen television at the bar downstairs at Ocean Harvest while dining on their reasonably priced seafood. They feature live entertainment on weekends. The Cask 'n'

Cleaver has live entertainment as well, and a great view of the mountain, but no dance floor.

For a nice spot to talk and relax, there's Josh Slocum's.

RESTAURANTS

The most elegant restaurant in town is clearly Roget's. Their food is prepared with delicate sauces and served with fresh vegetables. Of course, it is not inexpensive.

Whisky Creek, Josh Slocum's, the Chart House, and the Cask 'n' Cleaver are all good for steak and seafood. The local favorite is the Mogul Steak House, where you can cook your own and partake of an excellent salad bar.

Fine oriental food at reasonable prices is available at Matsu. For pizza, don't miss Perry's and Giovanni's. Ocean Harvest serves by far the best seafood. If you stay late at the slopes, don't overlook Altitude 9000 across from the Main Lodge. Portions are large, and the food is good and reasonably priced.

LODGING

Mammoth doesn't give anything away, but has everything from luxury condos to dorms. With 25,000 beds, the capacity equals Vail's. To get accommodations at the condominiums, contact the several reservation services in town. They are listed at the end of this chapter.

The list of individual condominiums is nearly endless. Among the nicest, those at Snowcreek Resort are one- to three-bedroom units with beautiful views and a shuttle to the slopes. Prices range from $70 to $160. Close to Warming Hut 2 are Mountainback and Sierra Megeve. Expect to pay from $130 to $200. Directly across from the Main Lodge is the Mammoth Mountain Inn. It charges between $42 and $150 for condominium and hotel accommodations.

Aspen Creek and the Summit Condos are both within walking distance of chair 15, where lift tickets are available. Prices range from $75 to $180.

If you'd like to spend less, there are some alternatives. The Sierra Nevada Lodge caters to bus groups and charges from $36 to $80. A bed-and-breakfast inn, the Snow Goose costs from $45 to $90. The least expensive establishments include the Innsbruck Lodge and Nugget Lodge. Prices range from $10 to $60, and both are clean and comfortable.

ACCESSIBILITY

Most people drive. The majority of skiers arrive from southern California (anywhere from San Diego to Santa Barbara). From the Bay Area, the shortest route is Highway 50 to South Lake Tahoe to Highway 19 or Highway 89, both to U.S. 396. With good conditions, this route will take six hours. But snow conditions can make 80 to 395 an easier route. Greyhound arrives from the north and the south, and Mojave Airlines has daily flights from Los Angeles, San Diego, and some smaller cities. Mammoth gets congested at times, so plan to use the shuttle buses and private bus lines once you arrive.

LISTINGS

Mammoth Mountain Ski Area
Box 24
Mammoth Lakes, CA 93546
619-934-2571

Mammoth Reservation Bureau: 619-934-2528 or 800-462-5571
Mammoth Properties Reservations: 619-934-3933 or 800-227-7669
Eastern Slopes Reservation Service: 619-934-2502
Ski Time Reservation: 619-934-7583 or 800-462-5584

LIFT TICKET

$20

RESTAURANTS AND NIGHTLIFE

Rafters, Old Mammoth Road, 934-2537.
Whisky Creek, Mammoth Lakes, 934-2555.
Village Inn, Main Street, 934-2264.
Ocean Harvest, Old Mammoth and Sierra Nevada Roads, 934-8539.
Josh Slocum's, Main Street, 934-7647.
Cask 'n' Cleaver, 460587 Old Mammoth Road, 934-4200.
Roget's, Main and Minaret, 934-4466.
Mogul Steak House, 10 Mammoth Tavern Road, 934-3039.
Matsu, Highway 203 and Mountain Boulevard, 934-8277.
Perry's, Main Street, 934-3251.
Giovanni's, Minaret Village, 934-7563.
Altitude 9000, Mammoth Mountain Inn, 934-2581.

LODGING

Snowcreek Resort, Box A-5, Mammoth Lakes, 934-3333.
Mountainback, Box 1437, Mammoth Lakes, 934-4549 or toll-free
   800-462-5577.
Sierra Megeve, Box 378, 934-3723 or 800-227-7669.
Mammoth Mountain Inn, Box 353, 934-2581.
Aspen Creek, Box 378, 934-3933 or 800-227-7669.
The Summit, Box 1058, 934-3000 or 800-421-8240.
Sierra Nevada Lodge, Old Mammoth Road, 934-2515.
Snow Goose Inn, Box 946, 934-2660.
Innsbruck Lodge, Box 758, 934-3035.

SQUAW VALLEY

Squaw Valley is big. Very, very big—twenty-seven lifts, including a gondola and a tram. You don't ski slopes at Squaw; you ski faces. Instead of judging the difficulty of the slopes, they rate the lifts beginner, intermediate, or expert. And it's very easy to ski Squaw and never ski the same *lift* twice in a day.

With all this terrain, Squaw has great skiing for everybody, including some of the most challenging and most concentrated expert skiing around. And because chairlifts, gondola, and tram are so well coordinated, base-of-the-mountain waits can be avoided.

Squaw's only fault is its lack of personality—it's so vast that it's tough to get a feel for the mountain. Also, the rest of the facilities are lacking. The resort has lost some of its lustre since the Olympic games in 1961.

THE SKIING

Squaw covers five peaks. It has a well-designed lift system that clears skiers out from the bottom. Unless you're an expert, your best strategy would be to take the gondola early in the morning, and then ski the eleven chairlifts that start from the upper gondola house. This way you'll avoid lines, and the snow up top is usually better. An added benefit is the two restaurants located at the top of the gondola. But be warned—showing up at the gondola on weekends when it opens can still result in a half-hour wait.

Many beginners are able to ski the high-altitude shallow slopes of Easy Broadway, Links, and Bailey's Beach, located on Emigrant Peak. Intermediates should love skiing the easy moguls off the triple chairlifts Mainline and Goldcoast.

Red Dog and KT22, on the left of the mountain, are made to order for experts. Red Dog, a mogul skier's dream, is a nonstop challenge. Experts should be happy: the lift lines here are substantially shorter than anywhere else. The West Face is as tough as they come, and the East is no slouch. Olympic Lady has gullies, wide bowls, and people who like to ski them fast.

The backside of Emigrant Peak has some less challenging but also less-used expert and intermediate terrain, while the Big Cornice-Sunbowl runs will keep any expert working. Finally, just in case Squaw has not yet challenged you, try Siberia and North Bowl. They're so wicked that people have fallen off just peering down at the almost vertical drop.

Squaw gets the famous—infamous, really—Sierra cement. This powder, which can be wet and heavy, is almost always present at higher altitudes. You'll have to work hard—and bring waterproof clothes. The season starts in November and lasts through May. Snowfall averages over 400 inches.

Squaw attracts big crowds, especially on the weekends, when lift line waits easily top thirty minutes.

THE TOWN/NIGHTLIFE

Nightlife, restaurants, and lodging on the lake are discussed under Alpine Meadows, and all are easily reached from Squaw. The Chamois Lounge, a relatively quite bar with a small dance floor, is the site of the only nighttime action at Squaw Village itself.

LODGING

Squaw Village's main claim to fame used to be that it was inexpensive. That's no longer true. But the village is still complete and convenient. The Olympic Village Inn has one-bedroom suites for $125 a night, but during vacation periods add $50. It does have a nice view of the mountain, though. The Lodge is a little less expensive, but not much, and condominiums are similarly expensive. Squaw is currently building some more lodging at the base.

LISTINGS

Squaw Valley USA
P.O. Box 2007
Olympic Valley, CA 95730
916–583–6985
Central Reservations: 916–583–5585, or toll-free 800–545–4350.

SUGAR BOWL

Founded forty-four years ago with Walt Disney's money, Sugar Bowl today would make the king of family entertainment proud—it's a clean, inexpensive, fun mountain for the family.

Accessible only by gondola, it was long called "one of the best-kept secrets of the Sierras," although now they call it world-famous. Sugar Bowl is the smallest of the ski areas in the Tahoe region, but because of its prices and charm, it's beginning to gain in popularity. And with the popularity comes a loosening up of the atmosphere.

Retaining the friendly ambiance of a retreat with a touch of European flavor, it possesses a warm and helpful and fun-loving staff. The slopes won't challenge anyone beyond a solid intermediate, and the ski conditions are better over at Squaw so if these are crucial considerations, you shouldn't be at Sugar Bowl.

The single base lodge has dignified wooden rooms, and you'll be served fine Old World cuisine, schnitzel, bratwurst, and the like, at the restaurant. Le Grand Hotel, at the base of the mountain, is the best place to stay. Sugar Bowl was designed as a secluded getaway and is best used as such. The hotel has maintained its formality: ties and jackets are requested after 6:00 P.M., and no children under seven are eligible for the ski package.

MOUNT LINCOLN 159

THE SKIING

Sugar Bowl, not large by Sierra Nevada standards, is cozy. Mount Disney and Mount Lincoln, both lower than the surrounding peaks, comprise the resort, and as the peak is only 8,383 feet—a couple of thousand feet lower than Squaw—you might want to move to the bigger resorts if the snow starts melting.

But average snowfall is about 450 inches, and there is always a 5- to 7-foot base minimum. There's usually enough snow by February to last the season. You'll see that neither mountain is huge, and the runs are short, but even on weekends you'll never find any lift lines.

With eight chairlifts servicing the two mountains, there are many easy ways to ski down the 1,500-foot vertical drop. While the Mount Disney chairlift is superb for intermediates and novices, the only truly challenging slopes are located on Mount Lincoln. Silver Belt, once the site of a famous race, is a very tough trail, and experts will find it alone a good reason to ski at Sugar Bowl.

THE TOWN/NIGHTLIFE

If you had hopes of exciting nights at the casinos, forget using the gondola, the sole means of reaching the resort—it shuts down at day's end. Sugar Bowl is mainly for families who stay together and retire early. On some nights, the resort offers entertainment in the lodge, such as Tyrolean nights with singing and yodeling exhibitions. On weekends there's a band in the Broken Tip Room.

All the restaurants are along Highway 40. Tiner's Station Bar and Restaurant gets busy in the evenings and the Cheese Store is open for breakfast and sandwiches. The Redwood Lounge and Restaurant operated by the Donner Summit Lodge serves dinners for around $15, and also beer and wine. The Donner Ski Ranch also has a night-club, and cafeteria that draws mostly families. For a more lively evening you might want to go to Tuckee—about twenty minutes away.

LODGING

Le Grand Hotel has rooms with and without meal plans. A five-day package, including meals, ski tickets, lessons, and lodging, costs $329 per person for four in a room. Without the package, the same room would cost $100 a night. Besides the hotel, there are a few private homes on the mountain.

The Ski Inn Lodge doubles as a hotel and American Youth Hostel. Located right next to the gondola, it is a family-run, Swiss-style chalet. Meals are made to order. Hostel accommodations cost $7.75, while private rooms rent for $27 a night. The Donner Spitz Hutte, another Swiss chalet facility, is a great deal, just two miles down the road. Bunk and breakfast cost $12. With its own ski hill and good nordic facilities, the Donner Ski Ranch charges $10 for a bunk. The Donner Summit Lodge, the fanciest of the nearby hotels, charges $34 per person. For $33 a night, the Norden Store rents furnished rooms and supplies breakfast.

Once a set of military barracks, the Donner Spitz Inn rents dorm space for $10 to $15 a person. The Clair Tappaan Lodge, run by the Sierra Club, is a big, rustic, wooden lodge (Sierra Club membership isn't required). For $20.50, you get sleeping space and three very good meals.

ACCESSIBILITY

Sugar Bowl is the easiest ski area in Tahoe to drive to, but you must have your own car. No trains or buses go there. The airport at Reno is 40 miles to the east, and Sacramento is 90 miles to the west. San Francisco is 190 miles to the west. Sugar Bowl is just five minutes off Interstate 80, a major highway open at all seasons.

LISTINGS

Sugar Bowl Ski Resort
Norden, CA 95724
916-426-3651

LIFT TICKET

$15 weekdays, $20 weekends and holidays

RESTAURANTS

Tinker's Station, Highway 40, Soda Springs, 426-3410.
Donner Summit Lodge, Highway 40, Soda Springs, 426-3638.

LODGING

The Sugar Bowl Lodge, Norden, 426-3651.
Ski Inn Lodge, P.O. Box 7, 426-3079.
Donner Spitz Hutte, P.O. Box 8, 426-3635.
Donner Summit Lodge, Highway 40, Soda Springs, 426-3638.
The Norden Store, Old Highway 40, 426-3326.
Donner Spitz Inn, Highway 40, 426-3376.
Clair Tappaan Lodge, Old Highway 40, 426-3632.

Other Areas

SUN VALLEY, IDAHO

Sun Valley is one of the grandes dames of ski resorts. Ever since Averell Harriman came west in the 1930s and built his resort, it has been synonymous with western skiing. It offers fewer of the narrow, diving trails of Jackson or Snowbird, but has instead long slopes, often filled with moguls. The lively town of Ketchum, at the mountain's base, houses many bars and nightclubs.

World Famous Bald Mountain

Sun Valley

Much of Sun Valley resembles a period piece. The Sun Valley Lodge, centerpiece of Sun Valley Village, has black-and-white pictures of Marilyn Monroe, Milton Berle, and Sonja Henie on the walls, and looks much as it must have in the 1950s. Sun Valley still recruits many of its instructors from Austria. For a middle-aged, affluent couple, Sun Valley is the place to be.

Resorts tend to be built more elegantly these days, so Sun Valley may not seem as posh as it once did. Averaging a little less than 200 inches of snow a year, it's well below the total for its neighbors to the south. And, unfortunately, the resort is divided into several pieces; many condominiums and hotels are at one of the mountain's three bases, while activity centers around the Sun Valley Inn, several miles away.

THE SKIING

Sun Valley is now two and a half mountains: Baldy, which claims most of the trails, and Dollar/Elkhorn, which has the beginners' slopes. In the past, Sun Valley was faulted for its lack of beginner terrain, but Dollar/Elkhorn answers the critics. Graduating from these wide, packed, treeless hills to Sun Valley's slopes may be intimidating, since good advanced-beginner terrain is fairly scarce.

With a dozen chairlifts to serve Baldy's approximately fifty trails, lines usually aren't long, though the trails can get crowded. But with so many chairs it's simple to move from section to section.

The mountain has three distinct faces. Christmas Ridge divides Sun Valley into a north and a south ridge, each of which is skiable. Advanced beginners or struggling intermediates can manage Seattle Ridge on the far south side. The bowls served by the Mayday trail are intermediate or advanced terrain, depending on the conditions. Experts will thrill to Inhibition at the bottom of the bowl, one of the toughest trails around, with a particularly brutal bottom.

On the south side of the mountain are two valleys, Lower River Run and Warm Springs. River Run has many challenging expert trails, the best being Exhibition, with its steep, angling fall line and huge moguls. Limelight on Warm Springs is probably Sun Valley's best-known trail, angling down from the top of Baldy with consistent steepness and large moguls.

Although Sun Valley isn't actually any sunnier than most other ski areas, because of its many exposures the skier can follow the sun. Seattle Ridge gets the morning light, Christmas Ridge and Bowl get it all day, and Warm Springs has it in the afternoon.

The free Cross Country Ski Guide lists several areas with groomed trails, in addition to some nice back-country routes. The commercial outlets (trails and ski rentals) are: Wood River Nordic–Elkhorn (7.5-kilometer trails), Sun Valley Nordic (25 kilometers), Wood River Nordic–Bigwood (10 kilometers), and Galena Lodge Touring Center (25 kilometers, 23 miles from Ketchum).

THE TOWN/NIGHTLIFE

Ketchum is fun. On two facing blocks, you can find everything from ferny spots for young professionals to country-and-western saloons to local hangouts. And most of the bars serve good food. If you asked someone where to go for a burger, sandwich, or burrito, they just might say the Silver Creek Saloon. If you asked where to go for rock 'n' roll and dancing, they'd tell you the same thing. Next door at Whiskey Jacques you can eat pizza and listen to country tunes, and maybe do some dancing. For a more mellow evening, try Ketchum's only yacht club, the Cedars Yacht Club, and enjoy their seafood. Across the street on the corner is Slavey's, a bit yuppie, with entertainment on weekends. Locals make their own entertainment a few doors down at The Casino.

At the Sun Valley Village, Duchin's—as well as serving some of the best food in town—has dancing for the over-forty crowd. The Creekside Bar and Grill, one block from Baldy, has afternoon and evening entertainment. Thanks to its location, it's a busy little spot.

Two very good restaurants rely more on their menu than their bar— the Pioneer Saloon and the Christiana Restaurant. The Pioneer is a popular steakhouse with good food at reasonable prices. The Christiana Restaurant is known for its continental cuisine.

On the lighter and less expensive side, try the Konditorei in the village for reasonably priced sandwiches and salads. Barnacle Bill's Seafood Express, located in a train car, is a nice dive for seafood.

LODGING

The Sun Valley Lodge and Inn has been in existence since the thirties and remains a first-class establishment. Recently refurbished, it retains an Old World charm, and is just a brief bus ride from the slopes.

There are several condominium complexes near the village center that range from in-town to five minutes away.

The condominiums next to the slopes are far from the most elegant we've seen. Those in the International Village and Greyhawk are newest and thus probably the nicest. The Snow Run condominiums are the only studios with a fireplace. Although small, the Edelweiss is reasonable. Rates run $75 for a studio, $120 for one bedroom, and $230 a night for three bedrooms.

At the base of Elkhorn lie the Elkhorn Condominiums. Studios start at $80 a night, one bedroom costs $150, and three bedrooms cost $165.

The misnamed Aspen Inn sits at the base of Baldy. It has a one-bedroom-with-kitchenette deal that costs $60 for four people. Two bedrooms go for $85, and three bedrooms cost $100. It's simple, but a bargain. Next door, and a nicer place, is the Lift Haven Inn, where a one-bedroom unit that sleeps four with a kitchenette costs $55. Two bedrooms (sleeps six) cost $90, and four bedrooms cost $165.

Ketchum has a number of inexpensive, basic hotels. Rooms at Bald Mountain Hot Springs, with kitchens, go for $43 for one bed, $46 for two, and up to $58 for four beds. The Ketchum Korral Motor Lodge has log cabins with one bedroom and full kitchen for $95 for four people. Best Western is represented by the Christiana. It's pretty posh for a Best Western, and costs $68 for two, with $5 extra for kitchenette or a fireplace. The Tamarack, also in town, costs $72 a night for two.

A mile from the slopes and resembling a Ramada is the Heidelberg at $60 a night for a double room, and $75 for a fireplace, kitchenette with a bed and hide-a-bed.

ACCESSIBILITY

Getting to Sun Valley can be a challenge. From the East, it's easiest to fly to Salt Lake City and then take a shuttle flight to neighboring Hailey, or a six-hour bus trip. Airlines such as Frontier, United, and Western fly into Boise, a three-hour drive. On Saturdays, Western flies into Twin Falls (one and a half hours away).

LISTINGS

Sun Valley Company
Sun Valley, ID 83353
In Idaho: 800–632–4104
Outside Idaho: 800–635–8261

LIFT TICKET

$24

RESTAURANTS AND BARS

Barnacle Bill's, Sixth and Main, 726–3301.
Cedars Yacht Club, 205 North Main, 726–5233.
Christiana, 309 Walnut Avenue, 726–3388.
Creekside Bar and Grill, at Warm Springs Lift, 726–8200.
Duchin Dining Room, Sun Valley Lodge, 622–4111.
Konditorei, Sun Valley Mall, 622–4111.
Pioneer Saloon, 308 North Main, 726–3139.
Slavey's, Sun Valley Road and Main, 726–5083.

Whiskey Jacques, 209 Main, 726–3200.

LODGING

Heidelberg Inn, P.O. Box 304, Sun Valley, 726-5361
Ketchum Korral Motor Lodge, 310 South Main, 726-3510.
Aspen Inn, P.O. Box 79, Ketchum, 726-5500.
Elkhorn Condominiums, c/o Unlimited Condo Services, P.O. Box 1100, Sun Valley, 622-3094.
Bald Mountain Hot Springs, P.O. Box 426, 726-9963.
Warm Spring Resorts (handles nearly all the condos at the mountain's base), P.O. Box 228, 800-635-4404.
Heidelberg Inn, P.O. Box 304, 800-643-4400.
Lift Haven Inn, P.O. Box 21, 726-5601.
Tamarack Lodge, P.O. Box 2000, 726-3344.

TAOS, NEW MEXICO

There used to be a sign at the base of Taos's slopes that read: "ACH-TUNG! You are now leaving the American sector!"

And that sums up Taos's attitude pretty well. The effusive Ernie Blake, skiing legend and creator/director of the facility, has managed to impress his gracious European attitude on this mountain in New Mexico. The result is an attractive base area, clever extras like "martini trees" (Blake places vials filled with a potent martini at the bottom of select trees all over the mountain), and a worldwide reputation for demanding skiing.

Nestled away from the day-to-day world, the Taos Ski Valley will help you forget your worries—and your car. If you stay at the Ski Valley, you'll live and breathe skiing—aside from a couple of lounges at the inns, there's not much else. Taos is a serious mountain for

TAOS SKI VALLEY

Photo by Larry Case

serious skiers, but, thanks to the overwhelming good humor which pervades, it is not intimidating.

But along with European charms come European prices, and you may find lodging in the base village too expensive. Fortunately, there are a number of hostels and less expensive motels in Arroyo Seco, about seven miles from the slopes, and in the town of Taos, about eighteen miles away.

THE SKIING

Although Taos boasts a highly praised ski school, beginners will be frustrated and sore. Taos is best enjoyed by intermediates and experts. The Bambi-Whitefeather and Honeysuckle-Totemoff-Winkelried runs are the main "beginner" trails, but even the rusty intermediate may have trouble on them. And going from green to blue runs is quite a big step. The other major beginner trail, Rubezahl, is really only a fairly boring connector between the Kachina lift and the base.

Intermediates will really be challenged. The blue runs are wonderful and the blacks are very tempting. West Basin, Lower Stauffenberg, and Shalako are fun, wide bowls, while Porcupine and Powderhorn are demanding but still manageable.

Al's Run is another thing. It resembles a cliff with some bumps sticking out, and it's the first trail you see when you reach the ski area. Apparently so many people pulled up to Taos, saw Al's Run, and made a U-turn for home that Ernie Blake had to take down his funny "ACHTUNG!" sign and replace it with one saying "Don't Panic! You're looking at only 1/30th of the mountain." This terrifying trail runs under the main lifts, so all riders can witness often brilliant skiing—and some crashing.

Experts are also enthusiastic about Longhorn, Walkyries, Inferno, and the Ridge trails, which are open about 60 percent of the season and offer deep, dry powder.

You'll seldom have to wait longer than ten minutes for a lift. If you do, Blake has been known to serve coffee and doughnuts to the skiers in line. The crowd at the Kachina lift sometimes builds around 11:00 A.M., but even then it's a fifteen-minute wait at most. Also, the #6 lift is much more crowded than the #2 lift about fifty yards away—although they go to the same place.

Taos's weather is relatively warm and the season usually begins in mid-November and ends in mid-April. Annual snowfall averages 300 inches.

Who skis at Taos? You'll find some beautiful people tired of Aspen and Vail, though for the most part you'll ride the lifts with Albuquerque residents, Oklahomans, and Texans. Lots of Texans. The hot thing to do in Dallas and Houston, it seems, is to pile four friends in your car, leave after work Friday, drive all night, and hit Taos's slopes Saturday morning. After skiing all day Saturday and Sunday, you pile 171 everyone back in the car, drive all night Sunday, and report to the office Monday morning.

Although most acknowledge that Taos is well designed, many complain that the last fifty yards of Whitefeather, at the very base of the slopes, is murder. Navigating the steepness, the moguls (small though they are), and the congregated beginners can be quite hazardous. Since this is the most congested area of the mountain, Taos would do well to create a better "unloading" area.

THE TOWN

The town of Taos is an interesting cross between a pueblo and a McDonald's. There are the residents—Indians, Mexicans, cowboys, New York retirees, artists from around the world—and dozens of art galleries; lovely buildings; and some very fine restaurants. In the same town you have fast food, self-serve gas, and "real" Indian souvenirs.

If you're an art lover you may even forget you came to ski. Dozens of small boutiques feature local talent and artists of international fame—R. C. Gorman and Georgia O'Keefe, to name two, are well represented.

If you just want a drink, your options are limited but good. The Rathskeller in the St. Bernard is dark, warm, often rowdy, and packed from 3 to 5. It's *the* place to relax and tell tales about the day's skiing. For an after-dinner drink, head up the road to the more sophisticated Twining Tavern in the Thunderbird. The drinks are hot, and the top-name jazz gets even hotter.

Ogelvies and the Adobe Bar in town are the favorite digs of skiers and upscale locals. Ogelvies, larger than the Adobe, is perhaps less intimate, but you'll like the lovely fireplace, cozy sofas, and darts. The Adobe Bar has raw oysters and shrimp, features a live folk singer, a friendly crowd, and Watney's ale on tap.

There's only one nightclub in town—the Kachina Lodge. It has live music in the lounge nightly and a dance hall that often attracts some good rock 'n' roll groups on the weekends. Even the older folks hit the Kachina on the weekends for some dancing, and the atmosphere is friendly and innocent and fun, reminiscent of a high-school dance.

The food is predominately Southwest-style—tortillas, chili, rice and beans—but for such a small town, the variety of cuisine is impressive. Generally regarded as the best restaurant in town, the Casa Cordova, near Arroyo Seco, serves continental cuisine. It's also very expensive. The Chile Connection at the Tennis Ranch of Taos is the acknowledged leader in native Mexican food, but again, it's fairly expensive ($15 or so). Northern Italy is represented at The Fountain, romantically tucked away off the main plaza area, and The Landmark offers French and German cooking. Fagerquists', five miles north of town, has a menu that's a treat itself and the biggest margaritas. It serves chicken, catfish, and big steaks. Dinner at all these places will cost over $10.

But there are two cafés we recommend you don't miss—Michael's Kitchen and Floyd's. Michael's Kitchen, half-bakery and half-restaurant, serves a mean bowl of chili, and you'll be able to eat for less than $8, although it requires discipline not to buy a pastry or a loaf of bread. The question is, is Floyd's a diner or a bowling alley? The answer is both. It has cheap burgers, fries, pie, and some Mexican dishes, a smoky bar with pool tables, plus—and this is the real attraction—eight bowling lanes. If you want to run into some natives, this is the best place in town.

LODGING

The lodging at the base of the ski slopes is excellent, but you'll have to pay for it. With the "Learn to Ski Better" packages—seven days of lodging, twenty-one meals, six day of skiing, six lessons, and other extras for about $650 (per person in a group of four), you can get a good deal. Of the handful of lodges at the ski valley, all have saunas and Jacuzzis, plus a rare intimacy and friendliness. The Hotel St. Bernard, the Hondo Lodge, and the Hotel Edelweiss are the most convenient to the lifts, but even the "least convenient" lodges, like the Thunderbird, the Kandahar, the Innsbruck, the Rio Hondo Condos, and the Sierra del Sol Condos, are at most a few hundred yards away. The ski valley is small and compact.

Down the road a few miles are two good budget alternatives. The Abominable Snowmansion is a friendly youth hostel with spacious dorms and a lounge. Fifteen dollars gets you a bed, linens, and a big breakfast. The El Salto Lodge is rundown, but it's cheap—$12 for a room.

Tennis buffs will be in heaven at the Tennis Ranch of Taos, which is highly praised for its lovely architecture. The Ranch offers six outdoor and two indoor courts, a heated indoor pool, and a fantastic restaurant. Located midway between the mountain and the lodge, its price is also between that of the base lodges and the motels. A large group could turn it into a bargain.

You won't find anything grander in town than the Taos Inn, a national historic landmark, but it will cost you. A step down in quality and price are the Kachina Lodge (a Best Western), the Indian Hills Inn, the El Pueblo, and many more motels. For rock-bottom prices in town, try the Bunk and Save (a small, family-style dorm—$12 single) or the Snake Dance (ramshackle but fun—$10 to $20).

ACCESSIBILITY

Taos Ski Valley is about 18 miles northeast of Taos and 150 miles north of Albuquerque. Shuttles run between Taos and the Ski Valley frequently for $5, round trip. You can drop off your Avis or Hertz rental car at the Ski Valley at no extra charge. Trailways provides bus service to Taos. Most major airlines fly into Albuquerque, and a few charter flights are available from Albuquerque to the small airport outside Taos.

LISTINGS

Taos Ski Valley
Taos Ski Valley, NM 87571
505-776-2291

Taos County Chamber of Commerce
Drawer 1
Taos, NM 87571
Information: 505-758-3873
Central Reservations: 505-758-2525

LIFT TICKET

$20

BARS

The Rathskeller, in the Hotel St. Bernard at the base, 776-2251.
The Twining Tavern, in the Thunderbird Lodge at the base, 776-2280.
Ogelvies, Plaza Real, 758-8866.
The Adobe Bar, in the Taos Inn on North Pueblo Road, 758-2233.

RESTAURANTS

The Casa Cordova, Arroyo Seco, 776-2200.
The Chile Connection, at the Tennis Ranch of Taos on Ski Valley
    Road, 776-8787.
The Fountain, off Taos Plaza, 758-2121.
Landmark Restaurant, 102 West Santa Fe, 758-1022.
Michael's Kitchen, North Pueblo Road, 758-3981.
Floyd's, South Santa Fe Road, 758-4142.

LODGING

At the Ski Valley:
Hotel St. Bernard, 776-2251.
Hondo Lodge, 776-2277.
Hotel Edelweiss, 776-2301.
Kandahar Condominiums, 776-2226.
Innsbruck Lodge, 776-2313.
Rio Hondo Condominiums, 776-2646.
Sierra del Sol Condominiums, 776-2981.
Thunderbird Lodge, 776-2280.

Outside the Ski Valley:
The Abominable Snowmansion, Arroyo Seco, 776–8298.
The El Salto Lodge, Arroyo Seco, 776–2689.
The Tennis Ranch of Taos, Ski Valley Road, 776–2211.
The Taos Inn, North Pueblo Road, 758–2233.
The Kachina Lodge, North Pueblo Road, 758–9190 or toll-free 800–528–1234.
The Indian Hills Inn, Santa Fe Road, 758–4293.
The El Pueblo, North Pueblo Road, 758–8641.
Bunk and Save, La Placita Road, 758–8268.
The Snake Dance, North Pueblo Road, no phone.

JACKSON HOLE, WYOMING

If ski areas were judged like body builders, Jackson Hole would surely win any contest: 2,500 acres of terrain (four square miles) ripple over a vertical rise of 4,139 feet, the nation's longest. And what ripples! The resort offers some of the steepest runs around, along with enough flat terrain for beginners.

But in a competition based on fun after dark, Jackson Hole might not fare as well—nightlife is negligible. Also, the area has an annoying price scheme. Tram rides cost $2 a shot, even with a lift ticket, which itself costs $20 during most of the season. Advanced skiers end up paying $30 or more a day.

THE SKIING

People are drawn to Jackson Hole by the scenic beauty and stay because of the incredible skiing. Trails on the mountain never get crowded, and the beginner trails are great. The Eagle's Rest double chair takes you up only 330 feet, but the length of the run is 2,260 feet. Similarly, the Teewinot double chair ascends 425 feet, and has a length of 3,060 feet.

Experts have large areas to roam at Jackson Hole. The "trails" on the east side are long and wide-open. These runs, which drop several thousand feet, provide unparalleled opportunities to ski steep, open terrain—it's like skiing bowls at other areas. Because of the amount of terrain and the smaller number of skiers passing over the same area, moguls don't accumulate. But if you like skiing bumps, you'll find Thunder, off the Thunder chair, challenging. So although areas like Rendezvous Bowl have steep pitches, they're not as difficult as you might think. The truly daring head for Corbet's Couloir (when it's open), which starts with a fifteen-foot vertical jump. It's a quick turn, then another, and down the rest of the mountain and to the bar for a drink and your friend's adulation.

Unfortunately, Jackson Hole falls short on its intermediate runs. Blue trails with names like Union Pass Traverse and Solitude Traverse should clue you in on the fact that intermediates should expect some traversing. The area has only a half-dozen or so legitimate intermediate slopes. The best are off the Apres Vous lift. On the optimistic side, if the conditions are good, intermediates can tackle many of the expert slopes.

Lines never build up, except on the tram during peak periods, when the wait can reach thirty minutes. Unfortunately, no chair provides a solid alternative to the tram (a major deficiency during Christmas). If you haven't skied Jackson Hole for several years, you'll notice two changes in the tram. It doesn't make a halfway stop for intermediates anymore, and you can no longer make a reservation—it's first come, first served.

January is cold in Jackson Hole—just ask the moose who all come down from the hills to the valley for the winter. Despite much snow (450 inches a year), the wind and sun can turn the slopes into concrete. In February and March, the thermometer hovers in the teens and twenties.

THE TOWN/NIGHTLIFE

Grand Teton and Yellowstone, two of America's finest parks, are right nearby, making a wide variety of outdoor sports available. Rendezvous Mountain, home to the ski area, is close to Grand Teton, but since the road isn't plowed during the winter, you'll have to go through the town of Jackson to get to the mountain's base. Although the road to Old Faithful isn't plowed either, a local concessionaire runs a "snow coach" to both the geyser and the nearby lodge. You can see the springs in the afternoon, spend the night, and then take the snow coach back, all for about $80 for two.

Despite its natural resources, Jackson Hole hasn't progressed too far in cross-country skiing. While there are fifteen kilometers of trails at the cross-country center at the resort's base that lead into Grand Teton's trail system, the trails in the park are not always blazed, and there is no map at the ski center to help you navigate. The ski hut does not keep track of who is on the trails—you're entirely on your own. Given Jackson's cold temperature, high altitude, and avalanche possibilities, you really should know what you're doing before you go out on any extended runs. If you start at the south entrance to Grand Teton Park at Moose, you'll find a nice trail to Jenny Lake, or starting north of Moose on the left side of the road just before Cottonwood Creek you can ski to Taggart Lake.

Teton Village, so marked on highway signs, is the ski area's village. It consists of a half-dozen hotels with their accompanying bars and restaurants, clusters of condominiums, and several stores nestled around the base of the resorts, including a small, expensive grocery store.

The town of Jackson booms during the summer; in the winter, it's fairly quiet, except at night when the "Devil's Triangle" of cowboy bars play live western tunes. You can have a great time at the Cowboy Bar, the Silver Dollar Bar, and the Rancher Bar shooting pool, stomping your feet, and drinking hard. Get up your courage and go there; it's twice as fun as the village.

With more atmosphere than any place at the ski village, the Mangy Moose is the place to eat. The chicken is delicious, as are the steak, seafood, and salad bar, and the drinks are great. (We recommend Bailey's Avalanche.) Dinner will run around $8. The Sojourner, the Inn at Jackson Hole and the Alpenhof all have traditional restaurants. You'll have to drive to the following places: only minutes down the road, the Calico House serves excellent but inexpensive pizza and Italian food; the Vista Grande is good for Mexican food; and the Steak Pub, on the south Route 89, gets mixed reviews.

Jackson contains some large supermarkets, some very classy clothing stores and art galleries, and the usual trinket shops. Check out the arches made of moose antlers in the park in the town's center.

LODGING

The mix of modern hotels at Jackson Hole's base is unpretentious, and all are a short walk to the slopes. For a bargain try The Hostel, one of the nicest and friendliest student dorm operations around. Private rooms go for $30 a night, and The Hostel has a lounge in the basement. The Inn at Jackson Hole offers reasonable rooms at reasonable rates: $52 during low season, $59 to $69 during regular season. Perhaps a bit nicer, the Sojourner Inn offers the exact same rates. The Village Center and the Crystal Springs are two more modest places, with rates running $52 to $80 at the Center and $49 to $51 at the Springs during the regular season. (These are nightly rates; they go down substantially for longer stays.) The nicest hotel is the Alpenhof, which runs $78 to $110 during the regular season.

If you really want a bargain, stay in Jackson itself. The Antler Motel, Ranch Inn, and Western Motel all charge $32 for a single and $42 for a double. The Executive Inn lets you put two people in one bed for $30, and the 6–K Motel charges just $25 for one bed, $32 for two. The 6–K, run by ski racers and coaches, also offers larger rooms with kitchenettes at great rates. They aren't elegant, but they aren't bad, either, and they're inexpensive.

Jackson has a nice set of condominiums right on the slopes. Studios for two cost about $340 a person for a week during regular season; two bedrooms with a loft cost a group of four about $300 for a week. The newer units like White Ridge, Wind River, and Timber Ridge tend to be more luxurious than the older places like La Choumine.

The Teton Village Central Reservations service will make reservations for you at any of the hotels or condominiums mentioned above. If you call their toll-free number they will help you rent houses at Teton Village and will assist with transportation arrangements and the

like.

ACCESSIBILITY

Jackson has an airport of its own—Western Airlines offers connecting flights from major cities, and Frontier flies in directly from Los Angeles and Oakland on Saturday, and from Denver every day. The alternative is to rent a car at Salt Lake City and drive the five hours to Jackson Hole. This, however, requires decent road conditions. Bus connections can be made from Rock Springs, Wyoming or Idaho Falls. A bus runs back and forth to the city ten times a day for $1 each way.

LISTINGS

Jackson Hole
P.O. Box 290E
Teton Village, WY 83025
307–733–4005
Central reservations 800–443–6931

LIFT TICKET

$20 during "regular season"; $16 during "special season"; plus $2 for each tram ride.

BARS

Cowboy Bar and Restaurant, 25 North Cache, 733–2207.
Rancher Bar and Lounge, 20 East Broadway, 733–3886.
Silver Dollar Bar, 50 North Glenwood, 733–2190.

RESTAURANTS

Mangy Moose, Teton Village, 733–5913.
Alpenhof Garden Room, Teton Village, 733–3462.
Calico Pizza House, Teton Village Road, 733–2460.
Steak Pub, 3 miles south of Jackson on 89, 733–6977.
Vista Grande, Teton Village Road, 733–6964.

LODGING

In Teton Village:
The Hostel, 733–3415.
Inn at Jackson Hole, 733–2311.
Sojourner Inn, 733–2311.
Village Center, 733–3155.
Crystal Springs, 733–4423.
The Alpenhof, 733–3242.

In Jackson Hole:
Antler Motel, 50 West Pearl, 733–2535.
Executive Inn, 325 West Pearl, 733–4340.
6–K Motel, 48 West Pearl, 733–2364.
The Ranch Inn, 45 East Pearl, 733–6363.
The Western Motel, 255 South Glenwood, 733–3291.

MISCELLANEOUS

BUSES: The Jackson-Rock Springs Stage, 733–3133.
  Jackson Stage (Idaho Falls), 733–4033

SLEIGH RIDES: A ride from the Sojourner Inn to a heated mountainside cabin. Reservations: 733–6657. Through the Elk herd: rides continuously from the dead end east of Broadway. Turn left and go four miles.

YELLOWSTONE TOURS: TWA Services, 307–344–7311.

SNOWMOBILES: Ray's Snowmobile Tours, 800–292–0066.
  Moose Chevron Service Station, 733–2811.

CROSS COUNTRY SKI GUIDES: Sign up for trips at Jackson Hole Cross Country Center, 733–3560.

Photo by Tom Johnston